Mrs. Cubbison's BEST STUFFING COOKBOOK

SENSATIONAL STUFFINGS for POULTRY, MEATS, FISH, SIDE DISHES, and MORE

Leo Pearlstein
Lisa Messinger

SQUAREONE
PUBLISHERS

Cover Designer: Phaedra Mastrocola • Text Illustrator: Vicki Chelf
Interior and Cover Photographs: Western Research Kitchens
Typesetter: Gary A. Rosenberg • Editor: Joanne Abrams

Square One Publishers
115 Herricks Road • Garden City Park, NY 11040
(866) 900-BOOK • (516) 535-2010 • www.squareonepublishers.com

The recipe on page 109 is from *The $5 Chef Family Cookbook* by Marcie Rothman,
Prima Publishing, 1997. Reprinted with permission.

Library of Congress Cataloging-in-Publication Data

Pearlstein, Leo.
Mrs. Cubbison's best stuffing cookbook : sensational stuffings for poultry,
meats, fish, side dishes, and more / Leo Pearlstein, Lisa Messinger.
    p. cm.
Includes index.
ISBN 0-7570-0260-9 (pbk.)
1. Stuffing (Cookery) I. Messinger, Lisa, 1962– II. Cubbison, Sophie, b.
1890. III. Title.

TX740.P28   2005
641.8′1—dc22

                                                                2004022567

Printed in the United States of America

10   9   8   7   6   5   4   3   2   1

Contents

Acknowledgments

Our sincere and hearty thanks go to everyone who helped make this book a reality:

Sophie Cubbison, a pioneer in convenience food products, who created many of the original recipes using her Melba-toasted stuffing mix more than fifty years ago.

Everyone at Square One Publishers who worked so diligently to bring the book to print, particularly publisher Rudy Shur for his encouragement and advice; editor Joanne Abrams for her outstanding guidance; marketing director Anthony Pomes for his invaluable assistance; and special projects editor Elaine Weiser for her unflagging support.

Ron Parque, president of Mrs. Cubbison's Foods, for his more than twenty-five years of support, friendship, and guidance.

Gerry Furth, who for more than twenty years created recipes and serving suggestions along with making appearances on radio and TV.

Marcie Rothman, who after more than twenty years continues to appear on radio and TV to share Mrs. Cubbison's recipes, and who helped test the recipes that appear in this book.

The home economists and chefs of our Western Research Kitchens who developed recipes based on Sophie's creative guidelines.

The office staff at Western Research Kitchens—Rachelle Bugtong, Melissa Eagleson, and Violet Coto—who always help us stay organized.

And our families for their continuous love and support: Helen, David, Howard, and Frank Pearlstein; Joel Weiss, Joan, and Harold Messinger.

Introduction

If you love stuffing, you are far from alone. One national poll after another has shown stuffing to be by far the most popular part of holiday meals. However, as someone who truly appreciates this savory dish, you know that it deserves a place at your dinner table not just on the holidays, but all year long. Congratulations, you have just opened the most stuffed stuffing book of all time! Within these pages, you will find over 100 recipes, everything from comfort food classics to the most innovative stuffing recipes ever created—all easily made with stuffing mix. We'll show you how to deliciously stuff everything from poultry, to meat, to fish, to fruits and vegetables; how to turn your stuffing into showstopping muffins, loaves, and balls; how stuffing can "hide" in everything from fried chicken, to lasagna, to the pie you serve for dessert. And, of course, we'll show you how to turn your holiday stuffings into memorable masterpieces!

How did we get to be such stuffing know-it-alls? That's almost as simple as our easy recipes. Our pedigree is impeccable thanks to Sophie Cubbison, a true stuffing pioneer. You may know her as Mrs. Cubbison, the name behind the popular stuffing mix that has lined supermarket shelves for decades. However, Mrs. Cubbison is much more than a name on a product package. Sophie, a 1912 home economics graduate, was a brilliant baker, who was one of the first in the country to sell whole wheat bread and later Melba toast, made from her bakery's outstanding white bread. Soon, using broken pieces of her leftover Melba toast, she invented Melba-toasted stuffing mix, a uniquely seasoned blend that first drew raves and recipe requests from family and friends, and later saved generations of cooks the time and effort of making their stuffing from scratch. Sophie was one of the first to demonstrate recipes in supermarkets. She appeared on TV's earliest cooking programs. And she scoured the globe for the best additions to her stuffings. Most important to you, a stuffing aficionado, she helped create hundreds

of stuffing recipes. We've selected the best of the best from Mrs. Cubbison's archives, making this book a true treasure-trove for you and your loved ones.

Mrs. Cubbison's Best Stuffing Cookbook begins with a chapter of basics—guidelines and tips for using stuffing mixes to create stuffing casseroles as well as a range of other dishes. Included in this chapter are four recipes for basic stuffing side dishes—two for oven baking, one for microwave cooking, and one for top-of-the-stove cooking.

Next, in Chapters Two through Four, you'll learn how to pair stuffing with poultry, meat, and seafood to make a range of tempting dishes. From Classic Turkey and Stuffing, to a wonderful Italian sausage and fennel stuffing, to a perfect poached salmon with dill stuffing, these dishes are sure to become favorites in your home, just as they were in Sophie's.

Our memorable holiday gift to you is Chapter Five, "Stuffing for the Holidays." Here, you'll find stunners ranging from cranberry, maple, and almond stuffing; to yam and raisin stuffing; and even fruit-stuffed acorn squash. These are dishes that will do much more than decorate your holiday table. They will truly make every holiday meal a special occasion to be talked about for years to come.

Next, pack your bags for Chapter Six, "Regional and International

Stuffings." Whether you're looking for a classic New England oyster stuffing, a spicy Southwestern stuffing, or an Asian-inspired stuffing made with fresh shiitake mushrooms and fragrant ginger, you're sure to find a recipe to fill the bill.

Sophie Cubbison had a lifelong interest in good nutrition, so it wasn't difficult to create Chapter Seven, "Low-Fat, Fruit, and Vegetable Stuffings." Here, you'll find delights such as a cornbread stuffing prepared with applesauce instead of butter, as well as an apricot and brandy stuffing that relies on egg whites rather than yolks. And rest assured that these stuffings are as scrumptious as they are healthy.

If you've always experienced stuffing in the form of casseroles, Chapter Eight will change the shape of your dreams with "Shaping Up Stuffing." Amazingly easy to prepare, these superbly sculpted dishes, from loaves to croquettes, will add a new dimension to your dining table.

Lastly, Chapter Nine, "Stuffing in Disguise," will delight and surprise you as you learn how stuffing mix can be an indispensable ingredient in appetizers, entrées, and even desserts. Just try our sautéed mushroom quiche hors d'oeuvre with a scrumptious homemade stuffing crust, our crisp oven-fried chicken, or our maple yam pie, and you'll see that stuffing mix may be the most versatile ingredient in your cupboard!

What was Sophie's favorite piece of advice? Never make one batch of stuffing when two will do. At her table, and at ours, the stuffing always disappears faster than any other dish. Once you try the recipes in this unique collection, you'll understand why!

The**Story**of Mrs.**Cubbison**

ophie Cubbison was born to cook. Even as Sophia Huchting, the daughter of a German father and Mexican mother, she began learning the techniques that would eventually influence many generations of home cooks.

Sophie was born in 1890, and by the age of ten, she was already displaying talent in the family kitchen. At age sixteen, Sophie started to cook for the laborers at her father's ranch in California's rural San Diego County. With the help of an assistant, the talented teen cooked and baked for forty men in two "cook wagons"—horse-drawn mobile kitchens. Once or twice a day, as the harvest progressed, the horses clopped along, pulling the wagons to their next destination. Sophie prepared five meals a day, starting with breakfast at 5 A.M. Two of these meals were "sweet" breaks, and consisted of Sophie's exquisite homemade desserts. The bread Sophie prepared to serve with meals was called black bread, a forerunner of whole wheat bread, which she was among the first to sell in the United States. Her grandmother had shared the recipe for this delicious, nutritious bread with Sophie's father when he was growing up in Germany, and he, in turn, had taught it to Sophie and her mother.

Soon, Sophie decided to couple her talents with formal education—not exactly common among women in the early 1900s—in order to further her culinary career. In 1912, she graduated with a home economics degree from California Polytechnic School in San Luis Obispo, which would later become part of the California state university system.

In 1913, Sophie began dating Harry Cubbison. By the time of their marriage in 1916, Harry was supporting his invalid parents and Sophie was supporting her widowed mother. The couple searched for a business opportunity suited to her baking talents and his sales ability—a business that would allow them to support their families. After a $300 investment in baking equipment, including a mill that would grind their own 100-percent whole wheat flour, the pair opened a bakery in Los Angeles. Sophie baked Cubbison's Whole Wheat Bread three days a week. For another three days each week, Sophie visited delicatessens and markets, where, in product demonstrations, she familiarized the public with this little-before-seen food.

In college, Sophie's classmates had predicted that she would become a health food pioneer. Their confidence was borne out not only when she introduced whole wheat bread, but also when she was one of the first to open a health food store in connection with her bakery. Moreover, Sophie sold a caffeine-free beverage made from roasted barley and Mission figs, as well as offering a variety of soy products. In fact, she was one of the first in the country to manufacture soy foods.

Perhaps most significant to Sophie's eventual success, however, was her production of Melba toast, which was to be the cornerstone of her legacy. Melba toast was originally created by renowned chef Georges Auguste Escoffier, who sliced white bread very thin, and then heated it in a low oven until golden brown and brittle. Legend has it that the cracker-like delicacy received its name from Escoffier's business partner, hotel owner Caesar Ritz, who named it after Australian diva Dame Nellie Melba. Soon, the toast was featured on the menu of the Hotel Ritz in Paris and the Carlton in London—two of the hotels owned by Ritz and Escoffier—and other bakers began to produce their own versions of Escoffier's creation.

Due to Sophie's interest in health foods, she was one of the first

Sophie Cubbison's health food store offered soy foods and other healthful products.

to manufacture Melba toast—made with her bakery's excellent white bread—under a branch of her business called Cubbison Melba Toast and Cracker Company. By 1926, Cubbison's Melba toast sales were enjoying moderate success, but, before long, a big break came Sophie's way. The famous "Eighteen-Day Reducing Diet," which included Melba toast, had been prescribed for actress Ethel Barrymore by the Mayo Brothers Clinic. The diet was printed by most of the leading newspapers in the United States, and soon, the demand for Melba toast became so great that the Cubbisons needed to operate three plants day and night to meet their orders.

Sophie loved the texture and health attributes of Melba toast. Since she was enveloped in a virtual mountain of Melba toast, she soon began experimenting with the leftover pieces of the product, deliciously seasoning it

and using it in place of bread crumbs in a variety of recipes, including stuffing. Sophie soon created her own stuffing mix—essentially, her Melba toast and a careful mix of seasonings—and for a number of years, Sophie served her unique stuffing at home, and fielded recipe requests from family and friends. Everyone not only loved the taste of the stuffing, but was impressed by the convenience afforded by Sophie's expertly flavored mix.

In 1948, Sophie introduced the stuffing mix as part of her product line and since then, many millions of boxes of stuffing mix have been sold each year. As a testament to her talent, ingenuity, and vision, Sophie's original recipe has not been changed. Bakers still follow her instructions as they prepare thousands of fresh, specially formulated loaves of white bread and cornbread daily.

Sophie Cubbison's supermarket demonstrations introduced her products to the public.

And consumers still enjoy and praise the stuffing, just as Mrs. Cubbison's friends and family did so long ago.

Although Mrs. Cubbison is no longer with us, her legacy lives on both in her famous stuffing mix and in this first-ever Mrs. Cubbison's cookbook. Our hope is that it will make your kitchen as inviting as Sophie's always was.

1.The**Basics**

History tells us that stuffing has been a much-loved food since the Middle Ages. For hundreds of years, of course, the making of bread stuffings was a time-consuming process. To start, you had to bake suitable loaves of bread, cool them, and either cube the bread or tear it into crumbs—a process that took hours. If you wanted the delicious flavor of toasted bread, that added another step. And all of this had to be accomplished before you could even begin adding seasonings and other ingredients.

The introduction of prepared stuffing mixes revolutionized the creation of this centuries-old favorite. No longer was there a need to bake, cool, and cube. In fact, you didn't even have to fiddle with seasonings if you didn't want to. Most important, as cooks throughout the last few decades have found, the only thing you lose when using these mixes is the inconvenience. As long as you follow a few simple "rules," the results are always delicious.

This chapter begins by introducing you to some basic guidelines for using stuffing mixes. It then provides four basic stuffing recipes—two for use in the oven, one for saucepan cooking, and one for microwave cooking. Although each of these recipes is wonderfully easy to follow, each results in a delectable side dish that can be paired with the entrée of your choice to create a memorable meal. Mrs. Cubbison would approve!

TIPS FOR STUFFING SUCCESS

Over the years, Sophie Cubbison and consulting chefs have used stuffing mixes to prepare literally hundreds of dishes, from basic stuffing side dishes to gourmet appetizers, entrées, and more. While it's not at all tricky to cook with stuffing mixes, we have found that the best results are achieved when certain guidelines are kept in mind. Follow these simple rules when using the recipes in this book, and you'll always enjoy stuffing success.

❏ For ease and consistency, all of the recipes in this book give stuffing mix measurements in cups. When purchasing stuffing mix, though, keep in mind that a 6-ounce package is equal to 3 cups.

❏ In our recipes, we refer to two different types of stuffing mixes: "cornbread stuffing mix" and "seasoned stuffing mix." Exactly what's the difference? The cornbread stuffing mix uses a bread made from both wheat flower and cornmeal, while the seasoned stuffing mix uses a bread made from only wheat flour. Often, these two mixes—both of which are seasoned—can be used interchangeably. However, the cornmeal in cornbread stuffing gives it a slightly sweet flavor and a somewhat gritty texture. That's why there are some recipes in which one or the other stuffing is a better choice. Our easy

tamales recipe, for instance, uses the cornbread stuffing mix to replace masa (corn flour), which is used in a more traditional recipe. Keep this in mind before you decide to substitute one type of stuffing for another.

❏ Both of the stuffing mixes we use in the book contain coarse bread crumbs rather than bread cubes. Nevertheless, cubed stuffing mixes may be used in any of our casserole recipes or to stuff a turkey. If, however, you choose to use cubed stuffing in a recipe in which the stuffing mix is used to replace bread crumbs, as in our deviled chicken legs, you will have to first crush the cubes into crumbs with a rolling pin.

❏ In each recipe, we suggest an amount of liquid that we feel gives outstanding results. However, these amounts can be adjusted according to personal preferences. If you like a moister stuffing, by all means, increase the amount of liquid until you achieve the consistency that you like.

When stuffing a turkey, remember that its juices will add some moisture, so unless you like a very moist stuffing, try reducing the liquid by as much as $\frac{1}{3}$ cup. Keep in mind that self-basting turkeys may result in even moister stuffing, as internal basting—which usually consists of flavoring, broth, and oil—is sometimes added to the birds to help keep breast meat juicy.

❑ Depending on your preference, butter, margarine, and vegetable oil may be used interchangeably when preparing stuffing recipes. Although we believe that butter adds the richest flavor, the use of margarine will not significantly affect the taste. Vegetable oil is fine, but is not our first choice unless noted.

❑ You will note that some of our recipes do not direct you to sauté vegetables before adding them to the stuffing mix. Although the vegetables will cook sufficiently when the stuffing is baked or otherwise cooked, you can impart a richer flavor to the stuffing by sautéing the vegetables before stirring them into the mixture. Note that it is *always* necessary to sauté meat before adding it to the stuffing.

❑ When following a recipe in which butter, margarine, or oil is used to prepare the stuffing mix, we recommend greasing the casserole dish lightly. If the recipe does not call for these ingredients, you'll want to grease the dish liberally to prevent sticking.

❑ As a general rule, a 2-quart casserole dish of stuffing should be baked covered at 350°F for 20 to 30 minutes, while a 2½- to 3-quart dish should be baked for 30 to 40 minutes, after which both dishes may, if desired, be uncovered and baked for an additional 10 to 15 minutes. This will produce a casserole that is hot and moist inside, with a temptingly crisp crust. If you decide to use a microwave oven to prepare the stuffing but you still want a crisp crust, transfer the cooked stuffing to an oven-safe casserole dish and place uncovered under a preheated broiler for 3 minutes, or until the topping is to your liking. This technique can also be used when reheating prepared stuffing.

❑ Generally, you can plan on ¾ cup to 1 cup of cooked stuffing for each person. This amount should be increased for heartier appetites.

❑ If any stuffing is left over from a meal, promptly cover and refrigerate, using the stuffing up within two days. Freezing is not recommended, as both the fluffy texture and the flavor of the seasonings will be lost.

❑ Although the recipes in this book were designed for use with Mrs. Cubbison's stuffing mixes, they will work well with any brand of traditional stuffing mix—that is, any stuffing mix that is essentially composed of bread and seasonings. You will, however, want to avoid side-dish stuffing mixes. Because these products contain broth and heavy seasonings, they will not work well in our recipes.

Stuffing or Dressing?

Although everybody agrees that it's scrumptious—and some consider it the best part of a holiday meal—everyone *doesn't* agree on what to call it. While some people refer to it as stuffing, others call it dressing. And still other people are confused, wondering if these two terms actually refer to different dishes.

We're happy to put this speculation to rest. There is no difference! Popular conjecture has been that perhaps it is called stuffing when it is stuffed into something like a turkey, and dressing when it is served on the side, but the actual distinction is an outdated, somewhat silly Victorian convention.

The earliest known term used to describe stuffing was the French word *farce,* meaning to stuff. For many years, the words *farce* and *forcemeat* were both commonly applied to a spiced chopped meat mixture.

The word *stuffing* first appeared in English print in 1538, and quickly became popular. Then, some time around the late 1800s, things changed. It seems that the term stuffing did not appeal to the Victorian upper crust, so the very proper people of the time began calling it *dressing.*

Nowadays, the two terms are used interchangeably, with stuffing being the term of preference in the southern and eastern portions of the United States. In this book, for consistency, we use the word stuffing except when a recipe is commonly known as a dressing. Either way, it's delicious!

CLASSIC OVEN-BAKED STUFFING

*If you like your stuffing to have a golden brown crisp topping
and a lusciously moist interior, this is the recipe for you!*

YIELD: 4 SERVINGS

1. Preheat the oven to 350°F. Lightly grease a 2-quart casserole dish, and set aside.

2. In a large bowl, combine the stuffing mix with the celery, onion, and butter or margarine. Gradually stir in the broth, fruit juice, or water until well mixed.

3. Transfer the stuffing to the prepared casserole dish, cover, and bake for 20 to 30 minutes. If a crisp top is desired, uncover the dish and bake for 10 additional minutes.

3 cups seasoned or cornbread stuffing mix

3/4 cup chopped celery

1/2 cup chopped onion

1/2 cup melted butter or margarine

3/4 cup broth, fruit juice, or water

LIGHTOVEN-BAKED**STUFFING**

*Looking for an oven-baked stuffing that's lighter on fat
and calories? This version may be light on fat,
but it doesn't stint on flavor.*

YIELD: **4 SERVINGS**

3 cups seasoned or
cornbread stuffing mix

3/4 cup chopped celery

1/2 cup chopped onion

1/4 cup melted butter
or margarine

3/4 cup broth, fruit juice,
or water

1. Preheat the oven to 350°F. Lightly grease a 2-quart casserole dish, and set aside.

2. In a large bowl, combine the stuffing mix with the celery, onion, and butter or margarine. Gradually stir in the broth, fruit juice, or water until well mixed.

3. Transfer the stuffing to the prepared casserole dish, cover, and bake for 20 to 30 minutes. If a crisp top is desired, uncover the dish and bake for 10 additional minutes.

BASIC SAUCEPAN STUFFING

Wonderfully easy to make, this delicious
saucepan stuffing is also low in fat.

YIELD: 4 SERVINGS

1. Place the butter or margarine in a large saucepan, and melt over medium heat. Add the celery and onion, and sauté for about 5 minutes, or until the onion is soft.

2. Add the broth, fruit juice, or water to the saucepan, and bring to a boil over high heat. Cover the saucepan, reduce the heat, and simmer for 3 minutes.

3. Remove the saucepan from the heat, and stir in the stuffing mix. Cover and let stand for 3 to 5 minutes, or until the liquid has been absorbed. Fluff with a fork before serving.

2 tablespoons butter or margarine

1/2 cup finely chopped celery

1/2 cup finely chopped onion

1 1/3 cups broth, fruit juice, or water

3 cups seasoned or cornbread stuffing mix

BASICMICROWAVESTUFFING

Microwaves not only are fast but also help preserve the moistness of foods—a big plus when you want to enjoy a quick dish of luscious stuffing!

YIELD: 4 SERVINGS

1 ¼ cups broth, fruit juice, or water

½ cup finely chopped celery

½ cup finely chopped onion

¼ cup butter or margarine

3 cups seasoned or cornbread stuffing mix

1. Place the broth, fruit juice, or water; celery; onion; and butter or margarine in a 2-quart microwave-safe casserole dish. Cover and heat on high (100-percent) power for 4 minutes, or until boiling. (Note that cooking times may have to be increased or decreased, depending on the power of your microwave.)

2. Remove the casserole from the microwave oven and stir in the stuffing mix. Cover and let stand for 5 minutes.

3. Return the casserole to the oven and heat on high (100-percent) power for 1 minute, or until the liquid has been absorbed and the stuffing is hot. Fluff with a fork before serving.

2. **Stuffing** and **Poultry**

Poultry has had a long and illustrious culinary history in this country, and Sophie Cubbison has been an important part of that history. Whether she was pan-frying chicken to feed hungry ranch hands or developing her delicious stuffing mix, Sophie spent decades creating and sharing delicious recipes for turkey, chicken, Cornish game hen, and duck.

Our archives, therefore, are a treasure-trove of the best poultry dishes in American culinary history, and we are proud to open our vault to you. If you want to master the cooking of the perfect turkey, this chapter provides easy-to-follow instructions for roasting the ultimate holiday bird—complete with a delicious stuffing, of course. But the following pages will take you well beyond the classic roasted turkey with temptations such as Blackened Turkey Breast With Zesty Jambalaya Stuffing, Turkey Cornbread Hash, Pineapple-and-Ginger-Stuffed Chicken, and Roast Duck with Raspberry Stuffing.

All of the recipes in this chapter are a testament to the versatility of seasoned stuffing mix. This savory ingredient can mingle with chunks of poultry in a sensational side dish stuffing, serve as the foundation of a hearty one-pot meal, be used as a crispy coating for individual poultry pieces, or make a moist and delicious filling for all kinds of delicacies. Perhaps best of all, stuffing mix not only makes these dishes delicious, but also speeds preparation, allowing you more time to enjoy your creations with family and friends.

STUFFINGS

TURKEY SAUSAGE, ORANGE, AND PECAN STUFFING

Although pork sausage is a traditional ingredient in many stuffing recipes, turkey sausage is an equally tasty and far leaner alternative. And with so many types of turkey sausage now available, each with its own seasonings, it's a snap to vary this stuffing to suit your mood!

YIELD: 8 SERVINGS

12 ounces loose turkey sausage

3 cups seasoned stuffing mix

3 cups cornbread stuffing mix

1 cup diced celery

1 cup chopped pecans

$1/2$ cup diced onion

$1/2$ cup diced fresh or canned mushrooms

$1/4$ cup melted butter or margarine

$3/4$ cup orange marmalade

$1/2$ cup diced fresh or canned pineapple, undrained

$1/2$ cup applesauce

$1/4$ cup brandy

1. Preheat the oven to 325°F. Lightly grease a $2^1/2$- to 3-quart casserole dish and set aside.

2. Place a medium-sized nonstick skillet over medium heat. Add the sausage, and cook, stirring often to break up the meat, until the sausage has been browned and no pink remains. Drain well on paper towels.

3. In a large bowl, combine the sausage, stuffing mixes, celery, pecans, onion, mushrooms, and butter or margarine. Stir in the marmalade, pineapple, applesauce, and brandy.

4. Transfer the stuffing to the prepared dish, cover, and bake for 30 to 40 minutes, or until heated through. If a crisp top is desired, uncover the dish and bake for 10 additional minutes.

ZESTY**TURKEY**AND GRAPEFRUIT**STUFFING**

This dish marries healthful fruits with turkey and stuffing.
The result is a luscious side dish, sparked by the
refreshing taste of grapefruit juice.

1. Preheat the oven to 325°F. Lightly grease a 2½- to 3-quart casserole dish and set aside.

2. In a large bowl, combine the stuffing mix with the melted butter or margarine. Add all of the remaining ingredients, stirring lightly to combine.

3. Transfer the stuffing to the prepared dish, cover, and bake for 30 to 40 minutes, or until heated through. If a crisp top is desired, uncover the dish and bake for 10 additional minutes.

YIELD: 8 SERVINGS

6 cups seasoned or cornbread stuffing mix

1 cup melted butter or margarine

1 cup cubed cooked turkey breast

½ cup chopped pitted prunes

½ cup chopped walnuts or pecans

1 apple, peeled, cored, and diced

2 tablespoons grated grapefruit zest

Juice of 1 grapefruit, plus water or chicken broth to make 1 cup liquid

HERBEDCHICKENLIVERSTUFFING

*The rich flavor of chicken livers, paired with smoky bacon
and herbs, makes a memorable combination.*

YIELD: 4 SERVINGS

2 slices bacon, diced

4 ounces chicken livers,
diced

1 1/3 cups water

2 tablespoons butter
or margarine

1/4 teaspoon dried
marjoram

1/4 teaspoon dried thyme

3 cups seasoned
stuffing mix

1/4 cup chopped pecans,
toasted

1. Place a medium-sized saucepan over low-medium heat, add the bacon, and cook until crisp. Carefully remove the bacon from the pan, and drain on paper towels. Carefully pour off the bacon drippings, leaving a few teaspoonfuls in the bottom of the pan.

2. Add the chicken livers to the saucepan and sauté until done, but still pink inside. Watch closely, as the diced livers will cook quickly. Remove the livers from the pan and set aside.

3. Combine the water, butter or margarine, marjoram, and thyme in the saucepan, and bring to a boil over high heat. Reduce the heat, cover the pan, and simmer for 4 minutes.

4. Uncover the saucepan, and stir in the bacon, chicken livers, stuffing mix, and pecans. Cover the pan, remove from the heat, and let stand for 5 minutes, or until all the liquid has been absorbed. Fluff with a fork before serving.

ENTREES

TURKEYCORNBREADHASH

A "magnificent mishmash" is how Sophie described homey dishes like this hash, which artfully combines turkey, stuffing, and potatoes.

YIELD: **6 SERVINGS**

3 cups cornbread stuffing mix

2¼ cups chicken broth, divided

½ cup melted butter or margarine

½ cup chopped onion

1 tablespoon chopped fresh parsley

¾ teaspoon dry mustard

2 tablespoons butter or margarine

¼ cup chopped green onion

¼ cup chopped green bell pepper

2½ cups cubed cooked potatoes

2 cups chopped cooked turkey

Salt to taste

Freshly ground black pepper to taste

1. Preheat the oven to 325°F. Lightly grease a 2½ to 3-quart casserole dish and set aside.

2. In a large bowl, combine the stuffing mix, ¾ cup of the chicken broth, and the melted butter or margarine, onion, parsley, and dry mustard.

3. Transfer the stuffing to the prepared casserole dish, cover, and bake for 40 minutes.

4. Place the butter or margarine in a large skillet, and melt over low-medium heat. Add the green onion and bell pepper, and sauté, stirring occasionally, for 2 minutes, or until the vegetables are crisp-tender.

5. Add the remaining 1½ cups of chicken broth, prepared stuffing, potatoes, turkey, and salt and pepper to the skillet, and mix lightly. Cook until heated through.

CLASSIC**TURKEY**AND **STUFFING**

This golden brown turkey, bursting with savory stuffing, will make any holiday memorable. If you decide to make a smaller or larger bird, refer to the inset on page 22, which provides information on adjusting cooking time and stuffing amounts.

YIELD: 15 SERVINGS

12-pound whole turkey, fresh or frozen (thawed)

Salt to taste

Freshly ground black pepper to taste

STUFFING

6 cups seasoned or cornbread stuffing mix

1 cup melted butter or margarine

1 cup chopped celery

1 cup chopped onion

1 cup broth, fruit juice, or water

1. Preheat the oven to 325°F.

2. Remove the giblets and neck from the turkey, and rinse and dry the turkey inside and out. Sprinkle the turkey with salt and pepper inside and out.

3. To make the stuffing, in a large bowl, combine the stuffing mix with the melted butter or margarine, celery, and onion. Gradually stir in the broth, fruit juice, or water, and blend lightly.

4. Lightly spoon the stuffing into the neck and body cavities of the turkey, allowing for expansion during roasting. If you have extra stuffing, place it in a greased casserole dish, cover, and bake alongside the turkey for the last 30 to 40 minutes of roasting time. For a crisper crust, uncover the stuffing during the last 10 to 15 minutes.

5. Fold the turkey neck skin and fasten it to the back of the turkey with skewers. Fold the wings under the back of the turkey, and truss the legs together with string. This will help the turkey keep its shape during roasting, and will provide a neater appearance when serving.

6. Place the turkey, breast side up, on a rack in a shallow open roasting pan. (The pan should be no more than 2½ inches deep.) If you are using a traditional meat thermometer, insert it in the thickest part of the thigh next to the body, being careful not to touch the bone. If you are using an instant-read thermometer, it should not be roasted along with the turkey, but should be inserted only to test the turkey's doneness near the end of the cooking time. If your turkey has a pop-up timer, you will not need to use a meat thermometer.

7. Place ½ cup of water in the bottom of the roasting pan, and arrange a tent of lightweight aluminum foil, shiny side down, loosely over the turkey to prevent overbrowning. Place the turkey in the oven and cook, using a bulb baster to baste the turkey with pan juices every 30 minutes or so during cooking, and to remove pan juices if too much fat accumulates in the roasting pan. Remove the foil during the last 30 minutes of roasting to promote browning.

8. Roast the turkey for 3 to 3½ hours, or until a thermometer inserted in the thickest part of the thigh reads 180°F, and a thermometer inserted in the center of the stuffing reaches at least 165°F. When done, the thickest part of the drumstick usually feels soft when carefully pressed with thumb or forefinger, the drumstick moves easily in the socket, and the juices run clear when the meat is pierced with a fork.

9. Remove the turkey from the oven, and allow the bird to rest for 15 to 20 minutes before scooping out the stuffing and carving the meat.

How Big Is Your Bird?

The recipe for Classic Turkey and Stuffing on page 20 will enable you to roast a 12-pound turkey to perfection. But what if your turkey is larger or smaller than the one in the recipe? In that case, both the amount of stuffing and the cooking time will have to be adjusted. The following information will allow you to enjoy success no matter how big or small your bird is.

Adjusting the Stuffing

When mixing stuffing for use in a turkey, a good rule of thumb is to allow $1/2$ cup of prepared stuffing mix for each pound of poultry. What does that mean in terms of raw ingredients? The following chart will help you make just what you need. Note that two amounts are given for the last two columns—the melted butter and the liquid. In each case, you'll want to use the first amount to prepare a more traditional stuffing, and the second amount—which you'll find in parentheses—to make a lighter stuffing.

Poultry Weight (Uncooked)	Stuffing Mix	Chopped Celery and Onion	Melted Butter or Margarine	Broth, Water, or Fruit Juice
6–7 pounds	3 cups	$1/2$ cup each	$1/2$ cup (2 tablespoons)	$1/2$ cup ($2/3$ cup)
10–12 pounds	6 cups	1 cup each	1 cup ($1/4$ cup)	1 cup (1 cup)
15–20 pounds	9 cups	$1 1/2$ cups each	$1 1/2$ cups ($1/3$ cup)	$1 1/2$ cups ($1 2/3$ cups)
20–25 pounds	12 cups	2 cups each	2 cups ($1/2$ cup)	2 cups ($2 1/2$ cups)

If you decide to stuff your turkey with one of the many different stuffing recipes found in this book, note that the recipes which use 3 cups of stuffing mix will generally fill a 6- to 9-pound turkey, while the recipes that use 6 cups of stuffing mix will generally fill a 12- to 15-pound bird. All recipes can be doubled or halved as needed. Do keep in mind, though, that these are only guidelines. A stuffing that includes many other ingredients besides the mix—one that includes a pound of sausage, for instance—will fill a larger turkey. Also remember that cavity size varies from bird to bird even within the same weight range.

Adjusting the Cooking Time

If you buy a commercial turkey rather than one from a local farm, you will usually find a label or tag that provides precise roasting times for that particular bird. If not, the following table will give you general cooking times for roasting turkeys of different sizes at 325°F. Do remember, though, that a variety of factors—from your roasting pan to your oven—can affect cooking time. That's why, when determining whether a turkey is done, it's so important to make sure that a meat thermometer registers 180°F in the thickest part of the thigh, and 165°F in the center of the stuffing.

Turkey Size	Roasting Time
8–12 pounds	3–3$\frac{1}{2}$ hours
12–14 pounds	3$\frac{1}{2}$–4 hours
14–18 pounds	4–4$\frac{1}{4}$ hours
18–20 pounds	4$\frac{1}{4}$–4$\frac{3}{4}$ hours
20–24 pounds	4$\frac{3}{4}$–5$\frac{1}{4}$ hours

MEDITERRANEANSTUFFED TURKEYBREAST

Pine nuts and olives are just two of the ingredients that turn an everyday turkey breast into a Mediterranean feast.

YIELD: 6 SERVINGS

2 cloves garlic, minced

2 tablespoons chopped fresh parsley

1 tablespoon chopped fresh oregano, or 1 teaspoon dried

1 tablespoon chopped fresh thyme, or 1 teaspoon dried

1 tablespoon olive oil

2-pound boneless turkey breast half, butterflied and skin loosened

Salt to taste

Freshly ground black pepper to taste

¼ cup chopped black olives

1 ⅓ cups chicken broth

1 cup dry white wine

2 tablespoons all-purpose flour

2 tablespoons butter or margarine

1. Preheat the oven to 400°F.

2. To make the stuffing, remove the zest from the lemon, and set aside. Thinly slice the lemon, and set aside for use in seasoning the turkey.

3. Place the butter or margarine in a large deep skillet, and melt over low-medium heat. Add the leek, pine nuts, and reserved lemon zest, and sauté for about 3 minutes, or until the leek is soft.

4. Add the chicken broth to the saucepan, and simmer for 5 minutes. Remove the pan from heat, and stir in the stuffing mix. Cover and let stand for 5 minutes, or until all the liquid has been absorbed. Set aside.

5. In a small bowl, combine the garlic, herbs, and as much of the olive oil as needed to create a paste. Set aside.

6. Rinse and dry the turkey breast, and season with salt and pepper. Lift the skin from the top of the turkey, and rub the paste under the skin. Sprinkle the olives over the paste, and top with the reserved lemon slices. Replace the skin.

7. Carefully turn the turkey breast over, resting it skin side down, and spread the prepared stuffing over the turkey. Tightly roll the turkey up, and truss with butcher string. Transfer the turkey to a shallow baking or roasting pan, skin side up.

8. Roast the turkey for about 30 minutes. Then add the broth and wine and continue cooking for another 30 minutes, or until a thermometer shows the temperature of the turkey to be 170°F, and the temperature of the stuffing to be 165°F. Remove the turkey from the oven and allow to rest while making the gravy.

9. To make the gravy, in a small bowl, use your fingers to mix together the flour with the butter or margarine to form a paste. Set aside. Place the pan juices from the turkey in a small saucepan over medium heat. Add small bits of the flour mixture to the juices, whisking after each addition until the gravy reaches the desired thickness. Adjust the seasoning by adding salt and pepper to taste.

10. Slice the turkey breast and serve, topping each serving with the pan gravy.

STUFFING

1 lemon

2 tablespoons butter or margarine

½ leek, diced

2 tablespoons pine nuts

1⅓ cups chicken broth

3 cups seasoned stuffing mix

BLACKENED**TURKEY**BREAST **WITH**JAMBALAYA**STUFFING**

YIELD: **6** SERVINGS

2-pound boneless turkey breast half, skin removed

2 tablespoons melted butter or margarine

3 tablespoons Cajun spice blend

STUFFING

4 ounces Andouille or Polish sausage, sliced

2 tablespoons butter or margarine

1 medium onion, chopped

1 small green bell pepper, chopped

2 green onions, thinly sliced

1 clove garlic, minced

2 tablespoons chopped fresh parsley

3 cups cornbread stuffing mix

$1/2$ teaspoon chili powder

$1/4$ teaspoon freshly ground black pepper

$1/2$ teaspoon dried thyme

$1/8$ teaspoon ground cloves

1 cup chicken broth

This easy recipe—which allows you to serve turkey and a spicy dressing without the bother of stuffing the poultry—makes it clear that turkey and stuffing can be a year-round treat.

1. Preheat the oven to 350°F. Lightly grease a 2-quart casserole dish and set aside.

2. Rinse and dry the turkey breast. Brush with just enough melted butter to cover, and sprinkle with the Cajun spice blend.

3. Preheat a large skillet over high heat. Add the turkey breast and cook for 5 minutes, or until the first side is browned, but not black. Turn the breast over and cook for an additional 5 minutes, or until browned.

4. Transfer the turkey to a roasting pan, and place in the preheated oven for about 1 hour, or until a thermometer inserted in the breast reads 170°F.

5. When the turkey is beginning to roast in the oven, preheat a large skillet over medium heat. Add the sausage and cook, stirring occasionally, for 3 to five minutes, or until lightly browned. Remove the sausage from the skillet and set aside.

6. Place the butter or margarine in the skillet, and melt over low-medium heat. Add the onion, bell pepper, green onions, garlic, and parsley, and sauté for 2 to 3 minutes, or until the vegetables are tender.

7. Add the stuffing mix, chili powder, pepper, thyme, cloves, and reserved sausage to the skillet, and stir to combine. Stir in just enough chicken broth to moisten.

8. Transfer the stuffing to the prepared dish, cover, and bake alongside the turkey during the last 40 minutes of roasting. Cook covered for the first 30 minutes. Then remove the cover and bake for 10 additional minutes, or until the top is crisp.

9. Place the turkey on a carving board, and allow to rest for 10 minutes. Then slice as desired.

10. To serve, arrange the stuffing on a platter, and arrange the turkey slices over the stuffing.

TURKEY'N' CHEDDARCHEESE BAKE

*Well before supermarket shelves were lined with meal
"helpers" that turned meat or poultry into hearty casseroles,
Sophie was making them from scratch at home.
This recipe creates a mini-masterpiece out of leftover turkey,
frozen vegetables, cheese, and stuffing mix.*

YIELD: 8 SERVINGS

1¾ cups butter or margarine, divided

1 large onion, chopped

6 cups seasoned or cornbread stuffing mix

1¼ cups chicken broth

10-ounce package frozen mixed vegetables, thawed

8 thick slices cooked turkey breast

¼ cup all-purpose flour

2 cups milk

2 cups grated sharp Cheddar cheese, divided

Salt to taste

Freshly ground black pepper to taste

1. Preheat the oven to 350°F. Lightly grease a 3-quart casserole dish and set aside.

2. Place 2 tablespoons of the butter or margarine in a small skillet, and melt over low-medium heat. Add the onion and sauté until soft. Transfer the onion to a large bowl and set aside.

3. Place the remainder of the butter or margarine in the skillet, and heat until melted. Set aside.

4. Add the stuffing mix, chicken broth, vegetables, and 1 cup of the melted butter or margarine to the reserved onion, and stir to combine. Spoon the stuffing mixture into the prepared casserole dish, and arrange the turkey slices over the stuffing.

5. Place the remaining melted butter in a medium-sized saucepan, and heat over low-medium heat for 30 seconds. Stir in the flour. Then gradually stir in the milk. Cook, stirring constantly, for about 3 minutes, or until the sauce bubbles and thickens. Stir in $1\frac{1}{2}$ cups of the cheese, continuing to stir until the cheese melts and the sauce is smooth. Add salt and pepper to taste.

6. Spoon the sauce over the turkey, and sprinkle with the remaining $\frac{1}{2}$ cup of cheese. Bake uncovered for 30 minutes or until brown and bubbly.

Handle With Care

By now, most cooks are aware that care is required in the handling of all foods, including poultry, to prevent food-borne illness. Unfortunately, you can't see, smell, or taste the bacteria that can cause problems. You can, however, take the following steps to make sure that your poultry dishes are as safe as they are delicious.

❑ Always refrigerate raw poultry within two hours of purchase—one hour if the temperature is above 90°F. Cook or freeze fresh poultry within two days of purchase.

❑ When storing poultry, make sure that it is wrapped securely to maintain freshness and to prevent the juices from contaminating other foods.

❑ Ideally, thaw frozen poultry in the refrigerator, making sure that the juices do not drip onto other foods. Keep it in its original packaging and allow five hours per pound to completely thaw. For faster thawing, place the poultry in a leak-proof bag and submerge in cold tap water, changing the water every thirty minutes to keep it cold, and allowing thirty minutes per pound. Cook the poultry as soon as it has thawed. *Never thaw poultry at room temperature, and never refreeze uncooked thawed poultry.*

❑ To avoid cross-contamination, keep raw poultry away from other foods. After cutting raw poultry, wash your hands, the cutting board, the knife, and countertops with hot soapy water.

❑ When cooking poultry, use a regular or instant-read thermometer to check for doneness, placing it in the thickest part of the food, but avoiding the bone. Whole poultry should reach 180°F. Poultry pieces such as turkey breasts should reach 170°F. If poultry has been stuffed, the stuffing should reach 165°F.

❑ Place leftovers in shallow containers within two hours—one hour when the temperature is above 90°F—and refrigerate or freeze immediately.

❑ Discard any food left out at room temperature for more than two hours—one hour when the temperature is above 90°F.

EASYSTUFFED**CHICKEN**

Boasting a zesty basting sauce of ketchup and Italian dressing and a quick-to-fix stuffing, this impressive chicken dish is a snap to make.

1. Preheat the oven to 350°F.

2. To make the stuffing, pour the stuffing mix into a large bowl and set aside.

3. Place the butter or margarine in a medium-sized skillet, and melt over low-medium heat. Add the onion and celery and sauté for about 5 minutes, or until the vegetables are soft.

4. Pour the butter and vegetables over the stuffing mix. Stir in the orange rind and juice, and set aside.

5. To make the basting sauce, combine the ketchup and salad dressing in a small bowl. Cover and place in the refrigerator.

6. Empty the cavity of the chicken, and rinse and dry the chicken inside and out. Sprinkle salt, pepper, and garlic powder over the chicken, both inside and out. Place the chicken in a roasting pan, and spoon in the stuffing. Sew or skewer shut, and truss.

7. Place the chicken in the oven and bake for 1½ hours, or until a thermometer reads 180°F when inserted in the thickest part of the thigh, and 165°F when inserted in the stuffing. Stir the basting sauce, and brush it over the chicken 30 minutes before the end of the cooking time. Then baste every 10 minutes until the chicken is done. Let the chicken rest for about 10 minutes before carving.

YIELD: 4 SERVINGS

1 large roasting chicken (about 5 pounds)

Salt to taste

Freshly ground black pepper to taste

Garlic powder to taste

STUFFING

3 cups cornbread stuffing mix

¼ cup butter or margarine

1 small onion, chopped

½ cup finely chopped celery

Grated rind and juice of 1 orange

BASTING SAUCE

½ cup ketchup

¼ cup Italian salad dressing

DEVILED**CHICKEN**LEGS

*When Sophie's parents were courting in the late 1800s, deviled
dishes were highly popular. That's why Sophie was especially fond
of this delicious chicken dish, which has the punch of Dijon mustard
and hot pepper sauce, plus a hint of sweetness from brown sugar.*

YIELD: 4 SERVINGS

1/2 cup Dijon mustard

2 tablespoons vegetable oil

2 tablespoons brown sugar

2 cloves garlic, minced

I teaspoon Worcestershire
sauce

I teaspoon salt

1/2 teaspoon ground ginger

1/4 teaspoon freshly ground
black pepper

1/8 teaspoon hot pepper
sauce

8 chicken legs
(about 2 1/2 pounds total)

2 cups seasoned
stuffing mix

1. Preheat the oven to 375°F. Grease a 9-x-13-inch baking dish
and set aside.

2. In a small bowl, combine the mustard, oil, brown sugar, garlic, Worcestershire sauce, salt, ginger, pepper, and hot pepper sauce.

3. Wash and dry the chicken legs, and baste with the mustard
mixture, coating the chicken on all sides.

4. Place the stuffing mix in a pie tin or shallow pan, and roll
the chicken legs in the stuffing mix to coat well. Arrange the
coated chicken pieces in the prepared baking dish.

5. Bake for 45 minutes, or until the chicken is lightly browned
and a thermometer inserted in the thickest part of the
chicken reads 170°F.

PINEAPPLE-AND-GINGER-
STUFFEDCHICKENBREASTS

Stuffed chicken breasts are so elegant, and yet so easy to prepare.
And when the stuffing contains juicy pineapple, crunchy almonds,
and aromatic ginger, the dish is as delicious as it is impressive.

1. Preheat the oven to 375°F. Line a 9-x-13-inch baking dish with aluminum foil and set aside.

2. To make the stuffing, combine the stuffing mix, almonds, pineapple, melted butter or margarine, prunes, and ginger in a large bowl, tossing thoroughly but lightly. Add the pineapple juice and sugar, and mix lightly. Set aside.

3. Rinse and dry the chicken breasts, and make a slit down the length of each half to form a pocket for the stuffing. Sprinkle each half with the salt and pepper.

4. Place $\frac{1}{3}$ cup of the stuffing mixture in each chicken breast. Fold the skin around the side containing the stuffing, and secure with skewers or toothpicks.

5. Spread the melted butter or margarine over the bottom of the baking dish, and arrange the stuffed breasts over the butter, skin side down. Bake uncovered for 30 minutes, or until a thermometer shows the temperature of the chicken to be 170°F and the temperature of the stuffing to be 165°F.

YIELD: 6 SERVINGS

6 boneless chicken breast halves (about 5 ounces each), skin left on

I teaspoon salt

I teaspoon freshly ground black pepper

$\frac{1}{4}$ cup melted butter or margarine

STUFFING

2 cups seasoned stuffing mix

I cup slivered almonds

$\frac{1}{2}$ cup fresh or canned pineapple pieces, drained

$\frac{1}{4}$ cup melted butter or margarine

6 pitted prunes, chopped

$\frac{1}{4}$ teaspoon ground ginger

$\frac{1}{4}$ cup pineapple juice

2 teaspoons sugar

APRICOT-**STUFFED** **CORNISH**GAME**HENS**

Stuffed Cornish game hens look so impressive when each is placed on a diner's plate. These impress even more due to the sheen of their sweet apricot glaze.

YIELD: 4 SERVINGS

4 whole Cornish game hens (about 1 ½ to 2 pounds each)

Salt to taste

Freshly ground black pepper to taste

STUFFING

¼ cup butter or margarine

½ cup slivered almonds

1 cup chopped onion

½ cup chopped celery

6 cups cornbread or seasoned stuffing mix

1 cup chicken broth

½ cup chopped dried apricots

2 tablespoons chopped parsley

1. Preheat the oven to 425°F. Grease a 2-quart casserole dish and set aside.

2. To make the stuffing, place the butter or margarine in a large skillet, and melt over medium heat. Add the almonds, and toss with the butter until lightly browned. Remove the nuts and set aside.

3. Add the onion and celery to the butter remaining in the skillet, and sauté for about 5 minutes, or until tender. Add the stuffing mix. Then gradually stir in the chicken broth, adding only enough to lightly moisten the stuffing. Stir in the apricots, parsley, and reserved almonds. Remove the pan from the heat and allow the stuffing to cool thoroughly.

4. Empty the cavities of the hens, and rinse and dry inside and out. Sprinkle salt and pepper over the hens, inside and out. Then fill the cavities lightly with the stuffing, sew or skewer shut, and truss. Transfer the leftover stuffing to the prepared casserole dish.

5. To make the glaze, place all of the glaze ingredients in a medium-sized bowl, and stir to mix. Set aside.

6. Place the hens breast side down on a rack in a roasting pan, and roast for 15 minutes. Using tongs, carefully turn the hens breast side up, and spoon the glaze over the hens. Continue basting every 10 to 15 minutes, cooking the hens for a total of 45 minutes, or until they are tender and golden, and a thermometer inserted in the thigh shows a temperature of 180°F.

7. While the hens are cooking, bake the stuffing casserole, covered, alongside the hens for 15 minutes. Uncover the dish, and bake for an additional 10 minutes, or until the top is crisp. Serve the stuffing with the game hens.

GLAZE

²/₃ cup apricot nectar or orange marmalade

¼ cup melted butter or margarine

¼ cup honey

1 tablespoon lemon juice

⅛ teaspoon cayenne pepper

ROAST**DUCK**WITH RASPBERRY**STUFFING**

*Sophie always said that roast duck—which is elegant, yet simple
to prepare—was an ideal choice for intimate dinner parties.
Her fruit stuffing is a perfect complement to rich duck.
If possible, for truer fruit flavor, make the dressing with
a 100-percent raspberry spread rather than a sugary jam.*

YIELD: **6 SERVINGS**

5-pound whole fresh or
frozen duck (thawed)

Salt to taste

Freshly ground black pepper
to taste

¼ cup melted butter

STUFFING

3 cups seasoned stuffing mix

½ cup chopped celery

¼ cup chopped onion

¼ cup slivered almonds

½ cup melted butter or
margarine, divided

½ cup raspberry or
strawberry fruit spread
or jam

¼ cup water

¼ cup lemon juice

1. Preheat the oven to 375°F.

2. To make the stuffing, combine the stuffing mix, celery, onion, and almonds in a large bowl. Stir in the butter or margarine. Then stir in the fruit spread or jam, water, and lemon juice.

3. Empty and wash the cavity of the duck and sprinkle with salt and pepper, inside and out. Fill the neck and cavity with the stuffing, but do not pack tightly. Sew or skewer shut, and truss.

4. Place the duck breast side up on a rack in a roasting pan, and brush with the butter or margarine. Roast for 1 hour and 40 minutes, or until a thermometer inserted in the center of the thigh shows a temperature of 180°F. As the duck cooks, carefully remove the clear fat from the bottom of the pan with a large spoon and discard. Because ducks contain a great deal of fat, you can expect a good deal to accumulate. Let the duck rest for 5 to 10 minutes before carving.

3. Stuffing and Meat

Even as a girl, serving supper to ranch hands from her covered-wagon kitchen, Sophie Cubbison knew that variety was the key to keeping diners interested in meals. It's easy to fall back on hamburgers or meatloaf time and time again, but that can quickly get boring. Fortunately, even with the busy lives most of us lead, it's surprisingly easy to incorporate a variety of meats in your diet, as well as to create showstopping dishes that are so simple to prepare, they can be served even on weeknights.

This chapter presents a range of memorable pork, beef, and lamb recipes. If you have always limited stuffing to poultry meals, you'll be delighted with the many dishes that deliciously pair savory stuffing with meat. We offer a number of favorites, from a glazed ham stuffed with pineapple and almonds, to an herb-seasoned steak filled with spinach and onions. We also share delicious creations that include meat in the stuffing itself. If you think that only sausage can be used in stuffing, think again. Although we are pleased to include a classic Italian sausage and fennel stuffing, we also share unique dishes that lusciously join stuffing with bacon and scallions, barbecued beef, and even ground lamb.

So the next time you feel yourself stuck in that meatloaf-and-hamburger rut, flip through the following pages, and learn how stuffing can quickly turn an ordinary meal into an extraordinary event.

Quick Tips for Pairing Stuffing With Meat

There really aren't many tricks to stuffing meat. It's easy, and yet it makes a dazzling presentation, turning a simple meal into a sophisticated feast in no time flat. By keeping a few guidelines in mind, you'll be able to easily pair stuffing with your favorite cut of beef, lamb, or pork. Moreover, you'll ensure that your meat-and-stuffing meals are as safe as they are delicious.

❑ When purchasing lamb or pork chops in your supermarket or butcher shop, ask the butcher to make a slit, creating a pocket for the stuffing. Or, if you prefer, simply make the slit at home using a sharp knife.

❑ Have your butcher bone beef, pork, lamb, or veal roasts. This creates a perfect cavern for stuffing.

❑ When buying flank steaks, make sure they are thin and long, so that you can cover them with a layer of stuffing and roll them up jelly-roll style. Tie rolled steaks with string or secure with skewers.

❑ To make sure that meat and stuffing have reached a safe level of doneness, use a meat thermometer to check for the following temperatures:

- Cook ground meat until the temperature reaches at least 160°F.

- Cook beef and lamb roasts and steaks until the temperature reaches at least 145°F for medium rare, or 160°F for medium. Make sure that pork roasts reach at least 160°F.

- Cook pork, lamb, and veal chops until the temperature reaches at least 160°F for medium, or 170°F for well done.

- Bake a precooked ham until the temperature reaches at least 140°F.

- Cook raw sausages until the temperature reaches at least 160°F, and reheat ready-to-eat sausages to at least 165°F.

- Cook stuffing within meat to at least 165°F.

STUFFINGS

ITALIAN SAUSAGE AND FENNEL STUFFING

Here is a wonderful stuffing that blends the distinctive taste of Italian sausage with aromatic fresh fennel. This is hearty, homey fare at its very best!

1. Preheat the oven to 325°F. Lightly grease a 2½- to 3-quart casserole dish and set aside.

2. Place a large skillet over medium heat. Add the sausage and cook, breaking the meat up with a fork, until the sausage is brown and no pink remains. Remove the sausage from the skillet and set aside.

3. Melt the butter or margarine in the skillet, and add the onion, celery, and garlic. Sauté for 3 to 5 minutes, or until the vegetables are tender.

4. Add the stuffing mix, fennel, apple, parsley, and cooked sausage to the skillet, stirring to mix. Gradually add the chicken broth, wine, and egg, stirring until lightly moistened.

5. Transfer the stuffing to the prepared dish, cover, and bake for 30 to 40 minutes, or until heated through. If a crisp top is desired, uncover the dish and bake for 10 additional minutes.

YIELD: **8** SERVINGS

1 pound sweet or hot loose Italian sausage

½ cup butter or margarine

1 cup chopped onion

1 cup minced celery

2 cloves garlic, minced

6 cups seasoned stuffing mix

8-ounce bulb fresh fennel, trimmed and sliced

1 Granny Smith apple, peeled, cored, and diced

¼ cup chopped fresh parsley

1 cup chicken broth

½ cup dry white wine

1 egg, lightly beaten

BACONANDSCALLION
STUFFING

Bacon and scallions pair perfectly in this savory stuffing,
which is moistened with tangy, slightly sweet tomato juice.

YIELD: 8 SERVINGS

8 ounces bacon, diced

6 cups seasoned or
cornbread stuffing mix

I bunch scallions, chopped

I green bell pepper, chopped

I cup chopped celery

I cup tomato juice

$\frac{1}{2}$ cup chopped fresh parsley

1. Preheat the oven to 325°F. Liberally grease a 2$\frac{1}{2}$- to 3-quart casserole dish and set aside.

2. Place a medium-sized skillet over medium heat. Add the bacon, and fry until crisp.

3. Place the bacon and drippings in a large bowl. Add all of the remaining ingredients, and stir until the ingredients are well mixed and the stuffing is moistened.

4. Transfer the stuffing to the prepared dish, cover, and bake for 30 to 40 minutes, or until heated through. If a crisp top is desired, uncover the dish and bake for 10 additional minutes.

BARBECUED
BEEFSTUFFING

This hearty stuffing, featuring barbecue-sauced beef,
is true comfort food! Dry red wine adds to the full-bodied flavor.

YIELD: 8 SERVINGS

1 pound ground beef
$1/2$ cup butter or margarine
1 cup chopped onion
1 cup minced celery
2 cloves garlic, minced
6 cups seasoned stuffing mix
1 Granny Smith apple, peeled, cored, and diced
$1/4$ cup chopped fresh parsley
$1/4$ cup barbecue sauce
$1/2$ cup beef broth
$1/2$ cup dry red wine
1 egg, lightly beaten

1. Preheat the oven to 325°F. Lightly grease a $2^{1/2}$- to 3-quart casserole dish and set aside.

2. Place a large skillet over medium heat. Add the beef and cook, breaking the meat up with a fork, for about 10 minutes, or until no pink remains. Remove the beef from the skillet and set aside.

3. Melt the butter or margarine in the skillet. Add the onion, celery, and garlic, and sauté for 3 to 5 minutes, or until the vegetables are tender.

4. Add the stuffing mix, apple, parsley, and cooked beef to the skillet, stirring to mix. Gradually add the barbecue sauce, beef broth, wine, and egg, stirring until lightly moistened.

5. Transfer the stuffing to the prepared dish, cover, and bake for 30 to 40 minutes, or until heated through. If a crisp top is desired, uncover the dish and bake for 10 additional minutes.

MINTEDPINEAPPLE**STUFFING** WITH**GROUND**LAMB

Fresh mint and juicy pineapple are the perfect complements
to rich ground lamb in this slightly sweet stuffing.

YIELD: 4 SERVINGS

I pound ground lamb

3 cups cornbread
stuffing mix

I cup crushed canned
pineapple, drained

1/4 cup chopped fresh mint

1/4 cup brown sugar

1/2 cup melted butter
or margarine

3/4 cup pineapple juice

1. Preheat the oven to 325°F. Lightly grease a 2-quart casserole dish and set aside.

2. Place a large skillet over medium heat. Add the ground lamb and cook, breaking the meat up with a fork, for about 10 minutes, or until no pink remains. Discard all but 1 tablespoon of pan drippings.

3. In a large bowl, combine the cooked lamb with the stuffing mix, pineapple, mint, and brown sugar. Stir in the melted butter or margarine. Then add the pineapple juice and toss thoroughly but lightly.

4. Transfer the stuffing to the prepared dish, cover, and bake for 20 to 30 minutes, or until heated through. If a crisp top is desired, uncover the dish and bake for 10 additional minutes.

ENTREES

FIG-STUFFED BAKED PORK CHOPS

*The pairing of figs with stuffing and pork chops
is truly a blessed union of flavors!*

1. Preheat the oven to 350°F. Spray a shallow baking dish with nonstick cooking spray and set aside.

2. To make the stuffing, in a large bowl, combine the stuffing mix with the butter or margarine, onion, and figs. Gradually add the juice, blending lightly but thoroughly. Set aside.

3. Rinse the pork chops and pat them dry. Heat a large skillet over medium heat. Brown the pork chops in the hot skillet.

4. Arrange the pork chops in the prepared baking dish, and pile the stuffing on top of the pork, evenly dividing the mixture among the chops. Then cover with aluminum foil.

5. Bake for 40 minutes, or until the pork chops are thoroughly cooked and tender, or a thermometer inserted in the chops reads at least 160°F.

YIELD: 4 SERVINGS

Four boneless
1-inch-thick
pork chops
(4 to 5 ounces each)

STUFFING

3 cups seasoned or
cornbread stuffing mix

½ cup melted butter
or margarine

½ cup chopped onion

½ cup chopped dried figs

¾ cup apple juice

APPLE-AND-**BACON**-STUFFED CROWN**ROAST**OF**PORK**

6- to 8-pound crown roast of pork, made with two loins of pork, ribs attached

Salt to taste

Freshly ground black pepper to taste

I clove garlic, crushed

STUFFING

I pound ground pork

3 cups cornbread stuffing mix

2 Granny Smith apples, peeled, cored, and diced

6 slices bacon, cooked until crisp and crumbled

I cup fresh or canned corn kernels, drained

I cup chopped celery

½ cup apple juice or apple cider

½ cup melted butter or margarine

Apples and pork make a delicious team in this impressive pork dish. The marriage is further enhanced by the use of apple juice in the sumptuous stuffing. Note that the stuffing also contains ground pork, which is always trimmed from the bones when a crown roast is made.

1. Preheat the oven to 350°F. Line a shallow roasting pan with aluminum foil and set aside.

2. Rinse the roast and pat it dry. Season the roast with salt and pepper to taste, and rub with the garlic. Transfer the roast to the prepared roasting pan.

3. To make the stuffing, place all of the stuffing ingredients in a large bowl, and mix until well blended. Pack the stuffing mixture into the center of the roast. Then wrap the rib tips with aluminum foil and place a sheet of aluminum foil over the stuffing.

4. Cook for 2 to 2½ hours, or until a thermometer inserted in the stuffing reads 165°F. To promote browning, uncover the stuffing for the last 30 minutes of cooking.

STUFFEDWHOLE**HAM** WITH**APRICOT**GLAZE

For Sophie, stuffed ham was second only to stuffed turkey.
She loved the way the sweet and savory pineapple stuffing
of this dish complemented the smoky flavor of the meat.
The glaze—a simple one of apricot preserves—adds
a sophisticated touch with a minimum of fuss.

YIELD: 8 SERVINGS

10-pound whole smoked cooked ham, bone in

2 tablespoons whole cloves

½ cup apricot preserves

STUFFING

3 cups cornbread stuffing mix

¾ cup crushed pineapple, undrained

½ cup chopped toasted almonds

½ cup melted butter or margarine

¼ cup minced celery

1. Preheat the oven to 350°F. Lightly spray a shallow roasting pan with nonstick cooking spray and set aside.

2. Strip the rind from the ham. Rinse the ham, dry, and use a sharp knife to cut it into large 2-inch diamonds, cutting all the way to the bone.

3. To make the stuffing, in a large bowl, combine all of the stuffing ingredients until well mixed. Stuff the mixture into the ham pockets.

4. Transfer the ham to the prepared roasting pan. Insert a whole clove in the center of each diamond, and brush the ham with the apricot preserves.

5. Cover the ham with aluminum foil and bake for 1 hour. Uncover and continue cooking for 30 to 40 minutes or until the stuffing is crisp and the temperature of the ham reaches at least 140°F. Remove and discard the cloves before slicing and serving.

PORK**CHOP**AND**PEAR** CASSEROLE

In this casserole, slices of juicy pear make a dazzling companion to succulent pork chops and fruit-filled stuffing.

YIELD: 6 SERVINGS

3 Bartlett pears

Six boneless
1-inch-thick
pork chops
(4 to 5 ounces each)

½ cup butter or margarine

¾ cup orange juice

3 cups cornbread
stuffing mix

1. Preheat the oven to 350°F. Liberally grease a shallow baking dish with butter or margarine and set aside.

2. Core the pears, leaving the skin on. Chop 2 of the pears and slice the third, setting them aside.

3. Rinse the pork chops and pat them dry. Heat a large skillet over medium heat. Brown the pork chops in the hot skillet, then remove them from the skillet and set aside.

4. Melt the butter or margarine in the skillet, and add the orange juice and chopped pears. Simmer for about 1 minute.

5. Place the stuffing mix in the baking dish, and stir in the orange juice-and-pear mixture. Arrange the browned pork chops over the stuffing, and tuck in the pear slices between the chops.

6. Cover the dish with aluminum foil and bake for 40 minutes, or until the pork chops are thoroughly cooked and tender, or a thermometer inserted in the chops reads at least 160°F.

STUFFED**FLANK**STEAK
FLORENTINE

This Florentine-style stuffed flank steak is easy enough for a weekday meal, but so elegant that it will impress even the fussiest guests.

YIELD: 8 SERVINGS

1 1/2-pound flank steak

2 tablespoons vegetable oil

1 cup beef broth

1 cup dry red wine

8-ounce can tomato sauce

1 clove garlic, minced

1/4 cup chopped fresh parsley

1/4 teaspoon dried rosemary

1/4 teaspoon dried thyme

1/4 teaspoon dried oregano

12 fresh mushrooms, sliced

STUFFING

6 cups seasoned or cornbread stuffing mix

1 pound fresh or frozen chopped spinach, cooked and drained

1 cup chopped onion

1 cup melted butter or margarine

1 cup beef broth

1. Preheat the oven to 325°F. Lightly grease a 2-quart casserole dish and set aside.

2. In a large bowl, combine all of the stuffing ingredients. Set aside.

3. Rinse the flank steak and pat it dry. Then use a sharp knife to score the steak in a diamond pattern on one side, if not already scored when purchased. Place 2 cups of the stuffing mixture on the unscored side of the steak, patting it almost to the edges of the meat. Roll the steak up jelly-roll fashion, and secure with skewers or string. Place the extra stuffing in the prepared dish, cover, and bake alongside the stuffed steak for the last 40 minutes of baking time. For a crisper crust, uncover the stuffing during the last 10 minutes.

4. Place the vegetable oil in a large, deep ovenproof skillet over medium heat. Add the stuffed steak, and carefully brown it on all sides for about 20 minutes. Add all of the remaining ingredients except for the mushrooms.

5. Cover the skillet and bake for 1 hour. Add the mushrooms and bake for 30 additional minutes, or until the meat is thoroughly cooked and tender and has reached a temperature of at least 145°F, pouring in additional beef broth or water as needed.

BEEF AND BROCCOLI CORNBREAD BAKE

In this kid-friendly meal, ground beef is topped with vegetables and a crispy cornbread crust easily made from cornbread stuffing mix.

YIELD: **8 SERVINGS**

I-pound package frozen broccoli or green beans

I teaspoon lemon juice

I tablespoon vegetable oil

1 1/2 pounds ground beef

I tablespoon prepared horseradish

10.75-ounce can condensed cream of mushroom soup, undiluted

1/4 cup water

3 cups cornbread stuffing mix

2 tablespoons melted butter or margarine

1. Preheat the oven to 400°F. Liberally grease a shallow 2 1/2- to 3-quart casserole dish, and set aside.

2. Cook the frozen vegetables according to package instructions, just until crisp-tender. Arrange them over the bottom of the prepared dish and sprinkle with the lemon juice. Set aside.

3. Place the vegetable oil in a large skillet over medium heat. Add the beef and cook, breaking the meat up with a fork, for about 10 minutes, or until no pink remains. Stir in the horseradish and spread the meat mixture over the cooked vegetables.

4. Pour the soup into a small bowl, and stir in the water. Pour the soup mixture over the beef.

5. Use a rolling pin to crush the stuffing mix into fine crumbs, and place in a medium-sized bowl. Stir in the butter or margarine, and sprinkle the stuffing mixture over the casserole.

6. Bake uncovered for 15 minutes, or until the casserole is heated through and the crumbs are golden brown.

CORNEDBEEFHASHWITH CREAMEDVEGETABLES

*If corned beef hash brings back memories of cherished childhood
meals, jump on the nostalgia bandwagon and enjoy this dish:
a tasty corned beef hash-and-stuffing ring, filled with
vegetables tossed in cream of celery soup!*

1. Preheat the oven to 350°F. Liberally grease a 6-cup ring mold with butter, and dust with flour. Set aside.

2. In a large bowl, combine all of the ring mold ingredients. Spoon the corned beef mixture into the ring mold and bake for 35 minutes, or until firm.

3. During the last 15 minutes of baking time, prepare the creamed vegetables by combining the soup, milk, and curry powder in a medium-sized saucepan. Cook over low-medium heat for about 5 minutes, or until bubbly. Stir in the mixed vegetables and corn, and continue to cook for about 2 minutes, or until bubbles again appear.

4. To serve, loosen the edges of the corned beef mold by running a sharp knife around the inside edge. Place a serving platter over the mold and invert, allowing the ring to drop onto the platter. Carefully spoon the hot creamed vegetables into the center of and over the ring.

YIELD: 6 SERVINGS

RING MOLD

3 cups seasoned stuffing mix

15-ounce can corned beef hash

2 cups milk

1/4 cup minced red bell pepper

3 eggs, beaten

2 tablespoons chopped fresh parsley

1 teaspoon onion powder

1/2 teaspoon salt

1/4 teaspoon freshly ground black pepper

CREAMED VEGETABLES

10.75-ounce can condensed cream of celery soup, undiluted

1/3 cup milk

1/2 teaspoon curry powder

2 cups mixed frozen or fresh vegetables, cooked

1 cup frozen or fresh corn, cooked

HERB-**STUFFED**LEG**OF** **LAMB**WITH**MINTED**APPLES

This distinctive dish is surprisingly simple to create. An herb-stuffed leg of lamb is adorned with stuffing-topped minted apple halves, which take only minutes to prepare.

YIELD: 8 SERVINGS

6-pound leg of lamb, boned

STUFFING

3 cups seasoned or cornbread stuffing mix

1/2 cup sliced celery

1/2 cup chopped onion

1/2 cup chopped green bell pepper

1/2 teaspoon crushed dried rosemary

1/2 teaspoon crushed fennel seeds

1/2 cup melted butter or margarine

3/4 cup tomato juice

MINTED APPLES

3 Granny Smith apples

1/2 cup mint jelly

1/4 cup water

1. Preheat the oven to 325°F. Lightly grease a 2-quart casserole dish and set aside.

2. To make the stuffing, in a large bowl, combine the stuffing mix, celery, onion, green pepper, rosemary, and fennel seeds. Stir in the butter or margarine and the tomato juice.

3. Rinse the lamb and pat it dry. Loosely pack the stuffing mixture into the pocket created when the lamb was boned. Tie the meat together or fasten it with skewers. Shape any remaining stuffing into golf ball-size balls, place in the prepared casserole dish, cover, and refrigerate. Bake alongside the lamb during the last 40 minutes of cooking time.

4. Place the lamb on a rack in a roasting pan, fat side up. Roast for about 3 hours, or until a thermometer inserted in the center of the lamb reads at least 145°F.

5. While the lamb is cooking, prepare the minted apples by peeling, coring, and halving the apples. Set the apples aside. Place the mint jelly and water in a heavy skillet and cook over medium heat for about 1 minute, or until the jelly has melted. Carefully drop the apple halves into the jelly mixture, cover, and cook for 5 minutes, carefully turning once with tongs after 2½ minutes.

6. Slice the lamb and arrange on a platter. Surround the lamb with the minted apple halves, topping each half with a baked stuffing ball.

BACON-TOPPEDSTUFFED LAMBCHOPS

A painless way to add vegetables to your diet is to stuff luscious double lamb chops with tomatoes, green bell peppers, and onions. The chops' well-filled pockets are then covered with savory strips of bacon, which broil along with the lamb, adding a rich smoky flavor.

YIELD: 6 SERVINGS

6 double lamb chops
(about 8 ounces each),
with pocket for stuffing

6 strips bacon

STUFFING

3 cups seasoned
stuffing mix

I cup chopped, peeled
tomatoes

$1/2$ cup chopped onion

$1/2$ cup chopped green
bell pepper

$1/2$ teaspoon dried oregano

$1/2$ cup melted butter
or margarine

$3/4$ cup tomato juice

1. Preheat the broiler. Lightly grease a 2-quart casserole dish and set aside.

2. To make the stuffing, in a large bowl, combine the stuffing mix, tomatoes, onion, green pepper, and oregano. Stir in the melted butter or margarine and the tomato juice.

3. Rinse the lamb chops and pat them dry. Loosely pack the stuffing mixture into the pockets in the lamb chops. Place the extra stuffing in the prepared casserole dish, cover, and bake at 325°F for 30 minutes. Then uncover and bake for an additional 10 minutes, or until the top is crisp.

4. Slightly stuff a strip of bacon into the opening of each lamb chop so that the bacon is covering the slit as much as possible. Broil the chops for about 15 minutes on each side, or until the bacon is crisp and the lamb has reached a temperature of at least 160°F.

4. **Stuffing**and **Seafood**

ophie Cubbison quickly realized that there is more than one way to stuff a fish. She took many a glorious whole fish, stuffed it full of delicious ingredients, and let its succulent natural juices flavor the specially seasoned filling. On other occasions, she chose the simple but no less tasty route of slathering savory stuffing between moist fish fillets, or rolling up fillets to enclose a custom filling. Of course, Sophie also knew that many stuffings are wonderful when served alongside seafood, while others can be quickly turned into showstopping side dishes by the addition of delicacies such as oysters.

This chapter is a result of the many years Sophie spent ingeniously pairing well-seasoned stuffings with fresh seafood. As you'll soon learn, you can fill a sea bass with Parmesan cheese, white wine, and chives; flavor a trout with caper-and-herb stuffing; liven up any plain grilled or baked fish fillet with a sophisticated shrimp and crab side stuffing; or create an elegant lobster pie—a spectacular entrée designed to take your guests' breath away.

If these dishes sound out of your reach, or simply too fussy to fit into your busy life, relax. This chapter will show you just how easy it is to prepare delicious seafood meals. How many ways can you stuff a fish? Turn the page, and let Sophie show you how to turn your next meal into a seafood feast.

Quick Tips for Pairing Stuffing With Seafood

It's very simple to prepare delicious seafood meals—complete with savory stuffing, of course. Our first advice is to make friends with the folks at your local fish store so that you can get the freshest seafood possible, cleaned and ready to cook. Then follow these few guidelines and you'll soon be creating many a fish feast.

❑ When buying a whole fish for stuffing, ask your fish store or seafood market to clean the fish—that is, to remove the scales, tail, and fins; and to gut and butterfly the fish. Leaving the head on the fish is optional. It can, though, help the fish keep its shape while cooking, and it can help to make a splashy presentation on a serving platter.

❑ To help prevent a whole fish from curling as it cooks, prior to stuffing, score the fish by using a knife to make thin diagonal slashes no more than $1/4$-inch deep about $1 1/2$ inches apart along both sides.

❑ Although you can stuff a fish without seasoning it inside, you'll enjoy tastier results if you rub the inside with flavorings prior to adding the stuffing. One easy option is to season the interior meat with lemon juice—unless lemon juice is an ingredient in the stuffing—and sprinkle it with salt and freshly ground black pepper. At times, depending on your stuffing and side dish choices, bolder seasonings—cayenne pepper and garlic, for instance—may be more appropriate.

❑ After stuffing a fish, secure it with toothpicks or skewers. If desired, you can instead sew the cavity shut with a trussing needle.

❑ For best results, before cooking, brush the skin of the fish with melted butter, melted margarine, or cooking oil. This will add flavor and will help keep the fish from drying out as it cooks.

❑ Avoid overcooking your fish. A general rule of thumb is to cook the fish 10 minutes per each inch of thickness, but this can vary. The best and easiest test for doneness is to examine the flesh of the fish, which should be opaque rather than translucent, and should be easily flaked with a fork. If all else fails, insert a meat thermometer in the thickest part of the flesh. When done, it will read 145°F. Keep in mind, too, that even after the fish is removed from the heat source, it will continue to cook from the residual heat, so it's important to take the fish out of the oven, broiler, or skillet as soon as it's done.

STUFFINGS

OYSTERANDHERBSTUFFING

*The texture of oysters makes them a perfect addition to stuffing.
Shallots, mushrooms, and thyme add wonderful flavor, and bottled
clam juice infuses the dish with moisture while boosting taste.*

1. Preheat the oven to 325°F. Liberally grease a 2-quart casserole dish and set aside.

2. Place the wine or chicken broth in a small skillet over medium heat. Add the shallots and cook for about 3 minutes, or until tender.

3. In a large bowl, toss the shallots with the stuffing mix, celery, mushrooms, parsley, and thyme. Add the oysters. Then gradually stir in the clam juice, blending lightly.

4. Transfer the stuffing to the prepared dish, cover, and bake for 20 to 30 minutes, or until the mixture is thoroughly heated and the oysters are fully cooked. If a crisp top is desired, uncover the dish and bake for 10 additional minutes.

YIELD: 4 SERVINGS

2 tablespoons white wine
or chicken broth

1/4 cup chopped shallots

3 cups seasoned stuffing mix

3/4 cup chopped celery

1/2 cup coarsely chopped
mushrooms

2 tablespoons chopped
fresh parsley

1 tablespoon chopped fresh
thyme, or 1 teaspoon dried

8-ounce jar oysters,
drained and chopped

1 cup bottled clam juice

SHRIMPANDCRABSTUFFING

*Sophie was down-to-earth, but she loved easy elegance.
That's why recipes like this simple yet sophisticated
shrimp and crab stuffing were among her favorites.*

YIELD: 8 SERVINGS

1 cup butter or margarine

1 ½ cups chopped celery

1 cup chopped onion

6 cups seasoned
stuffing mix

½ cup chopped
peeled and deveined
uncooked shrimp

½ cup shredded crabmeat

⅓ cup chopped
fresh parsley

½ teaspoon freshly ground
black pepper

1 ½ cups chicken broth

1. Preheat the oven to 350°F. Lightly grease a 2½- to 3-quart casserole dish and set aside.

2. Place the butter or margarine in a large skillet, and melt over medium heat. Add the celery and onion and sauté for 5 minutes, or until the vegetables are soft.

3. In a large bowl, combine the stuffing mix with the sautéed vegetables, shrimp, crabmeat, parsley, and pepper. Gradually stir in the chicken broth.

4. Transfer the stuffing to the prepared dish, cover, and bake for 30 minutes, or until the seafood is cooked. If a crisp top is desired, uncover the dish and bake for 10 additional minutes.

ENTREES

PARMESANANDWHITEWINE STUFFEDSEABASS

In this dish, fragrant chives, Parmesan cheese, and onions add just the right zing to a sea bass stuffing.

1. Preheat the oven to 350°F. Liberally grease a baking dish and set aside.

2. To make the stuffing, in a medium-sized bowl, combine the stuffing mix, onion, Parmesan cheese, and chives. Stir in the wine, butter or margarine, and lemon juice.

3. Rinse the fish and pat it dry. Place it in the prepared baking dish and sprinkle the interior of the fish with salt and pepper. Stuff the fish with the prepared mixture and secure with toothpicks or skewers. Brush the outside of the fish with the butter, margarine, or oil.

4. Place the fish in the oven and bake uncovered for 40 minutes, or until the fish flakes easily when tested with a fork.

YIELD: 6 SERVINGS

4-pound cleaned whole sea bass or other fish

Salt to taste

Freshly ground black pepper to taste

Melted butter, melted margarine, or vegetable oil

STUFFING

3 cups seasoned or cornbread stuffing mix

1/4 cup chopped onion

1/4 cup grated Parmesan cheese

2 tablespoons chopped fresh chives

1 cup dry white wine

1/2 cup melted butter or margarine

2 tablespoons lemon juice

YIELD: **6** SERVINGS

4-pound cleaned whole trout
or other fish

Juice of 1 lemon

Salt to taste

Freshly ground black pepper
to taste

Melted butter, melted
margarine, or vegetable oil

STUFFING

3 cups seasoned or
cornbread stuffing mix

$1/2$ cup chopped celery

$1/4$ cup chopped onion

2 tablespoons chopped
fresh parsley

2 tablespoons chopped
capers

$1/2$ teaspoon dried tarragon

$1/2$ cup melted butter
or margarine

1 egg, beaten

$1/4$ cup chicken broth

CAPERANDHERB STUFFEDTROUT

*Capers add the perfect pungent accent
to this herb-flavored stuffing.*

1. Preheat the oven to 350°F. Liberally grease a baking dish and set aside.

2. To make the stuffing, in a medium-sized bowl, combine the stuffing mix, celery, onion, parsley, capers, and tarragon. Stir in the butter or margarine and the egg. Then gradually stir in just enough broth to moisten the mixture to the desired consistency. Set aside.

3. Rinse the fish and pat it dry. Place it in the prepared baking dish and rub the interior of the fish with the lemon juice. Then sprinkle with salt and pepper to taste.

4. Stuff the fish with the prepared mixture and secure with toothpicks or skewers. Brush the outside of the fish with the butter, margarine, or oil.

5. Place the fish in the oven and bake uncovered for 40 minutes, or until the fish flakes easily when tested with a fork.

SCANDINAVIAN
STUFFED**SOLE**

It's easy to enjoy a taste of Scandinavia. Just add
dill pickles to a savory stuffing, slather it on sole fillets,
and top with thin slices of tomato and onion.

1. Preheat the oven to 350°F. Liberally grease a baking dish and set aside.

2. To make the stuffing, place the butter or margarine in a large skillet, and melt over medium heat. Add the pickle and onion and sauté for 5 minutes, or just until the onion is soft.

3. In a medium-sized bowl, combine all of the stuffing ingredients, including the pickle and onion mixture, adding just enough wine to moisten the mixture to the desired consistency.

4. Rinse the fish fillets and pat them dry. Place half of the fish fillets in the prepared dish, and spread the stuffing over them. Top with the remaining fish. Arrange the onion and tomato slices over the fish, and sprinkle with the salt, pepper, and basil. The stack will measure about 2 inches high.

5. Cover the fish and bake for 15 minutes. Uncover and bake for 5 additional minutes, or until the fish flakes easily when tested with a fork.

YIELD: 6 SERVINGS

3 pounds fillet of sole
or halibut

I small onion, thinly sliced

I medium tomato,
thinly sliced

Salt to taste

Freshly ground black pepper
to taste

Chopped fresh basil
to taste

STUFFING

¼ cup butter or margarine

¼ cup chopped dill pickle

¼ cup chopped onion

3 cups cornbread
stuffing mix

I egg, beaten

⅔ cup dry white wine

SNAPPER**TERIYAKI** WITH**ASIAN**STUFFING

Marinades are an outstanding means of infusing fish with flavor. Here, red snapper fillets get the benefit of a delicious teriyaki marinade, including Dijon mustard, garlic, and fresh ginger, before being paired with an equally enticing Asian stuffing.

YIELD: 6 SERVINGS

1 1/2 pounds red snapper fillets

Toasted sesame seeds
for garnish

MARINADE

3 tablespoons regular or
reduced-sodium soy sauce

2 tablespoons sake
or sherry

1 tablespoon Dijon mustard

1 tablespoon peanut or
vegetable oil

1 tablespoon sugar

1 1/2 teaspoons sesame oil

1 1/2 teaspoons grated
fresh ginger

2 cloves garlic, minced

1. To make the marinade, combine all of the marinade ingredients in a shallow dish. Rinse the fish and place it in the marinade. Turn to coat thoroughly, cover, and marinate in the refrigerator for at least 1 hour, turning the fish once or twice.

2. Preheat the broiler.

3. When the fish is ready to cook, prepare the stuffing by combining the water, soy sauce, butter or margarine, and ginger in a medium-sized saucepan. Bring to a boil, reduce the heat, cover, and simmer for 4 minutes.

4. Carefully uncover the saucepan and stir in the stuffing mix, bean sprouts, and green onions. Cover and let stand for 5 minutes. Fluff with a fork before serving.

5. While the stuffing is cooking, remove the fish from the marinade, discarding the marinade. Liberally grease a broiler rack and place the snapper on it. Broil 2 inches from the heat source for 5 minutes, or until the fish is lightly browned and the flesh flakes easily when tested with a fork. Do not turn. Sprinkle with the sesame seeds and serve with the Asian Stuffing.

ASIAN STUFFING

1 1/3 cups water

2 tablespoons regular or reduced-sodium soy sauce

2 tablespoons butter or margarine

1/4 teaspoon grated fresh or powdered ginger

3 cups seasoned stuffing mix

1 cup bean sprouts

2 green onions, chopped, including tops

POACHED**SALMON**WITH **DILL**MUSTARD**SAUCE** AND**DILL**STUFFING

Poaching—cooking food in seasoned liquid just below the boiling point—is a good way to delicately prepare and flavor fish. This dish features dill stuffing and dill mustard sauce as subtle accompaniments to perfectly poached salmon.

YIELD: 6 SERVINGS

2-pound piece salmon

Lemon slices for garnish, optional

Fresh dill for garnish, optional

POACHING LIQUID

2 cups water

I cup dry white wine

I small carrot, thinly sliced

I small onion, thinly sliced

I small stalk celery, thinly sliced

$1/2$ lemon, thinly sliced

3 sprigs parsley

8 peppercorns

$1/2$ teaspoon salt

$1/4$ teaspoon dried thyme

1. To poach the salmon, place all of the poaching liquid ingredients in a fish poacher. Cover and simmer for 15 minutes.

2. Rinse the fish. Measure the depth of the fish at its thickest point to determine the poaching time. Then arrange the fish on the poaching rack and set it in the simmering wine mixture. After simmering resumes, poach 10 minutes for each inch of fish thickness, or until the flesh flakes easily when prodded with a fork at its thickest part, and turns pale pink near the bone.

3. Carefully lift the rack containing the salmon and slip the fish onto the serving platter. Peel and discard the exposed skin, and garnish with the lemon slices and dill.

4. While the salmon is poaching, prepare the stuffing by combining the water, butter or margarine, lemon zest, and dill in a medium-sized saucepan. Bring to a boil, reduce the heat, and add the corn and red pepper. Cover the pan and simmer for 4 minutes.

5. Remove the saucepan from the heat, carefully uncover, and stir in the stuffing mix. Cover and let stand for 5 minutes. Remove the cover and fluff with a fork.

6. To prepare the sauce, in a small bowl, combine all of the sauce ingredients, stirring well.

7. Serve the salmon hot or chilled, accompanying it with the sauce and stuffing.

DILL STUFFING

1 1/3 cups water

2 tablespoons butter or margarine

1 teaspoon grated lemon zest

1 teaspoon chopped fresh dill

1/2 cup canned corn, drained

1/4 cup finely chopped red bell pepper

3 cups cornbread stuffing mix

DILL MUSTARD SAUCE

1/4 cup Dijon mustard

1/4 cup mayonnaise

1/4 cup finely chopped fresh dill

2 tablespoons sugar

1 tablespoon white wine vinegar

ITALIANHALIBUTSTEAKS WITHSCAMPISTUFFING

YIELD: 4 SERVINGS

1/4 cup butter or margarine

1/4 cup white wine

I teaspoon dried oregano

I teaspoon grated lemon zest

1/2 teaspoon salt

1/4 teaspoon freshly ground black pepper

I clove garlic, minced

2 pounds (1-inch-thick) halibut steaks

SCAMPI STUFFING

1 1/3 cups water

2 tablespoons butter or margarine

I teaspoon grated lemon zest

1/2 teaspoon dried oregano

4 ounces peeled and deveined uncooked small shrimp

3 cups seasoned stuffing mix

The fruits of Sophie's travels couldn't be more apparent than in this recipe for Italian-seasoned halibut steaks.

1. Preheat the broiler.

2. To prepare the stuffing, in a medium-sized saucepan, combine the water, butter or margarine, lemon zest, and oregano. Bring to a boil. Then reduce the heat, cover, and simmer for 3 minutes.

3. Add the shrimp to the saucepan and simmer for 1 minute, or just until the shrimp turn pink. Remove from the heat, carefully uncover, and stir in the stuffing mix. Cover and let stand for 5 minutes. Remove the cover and fluff with a fork before serving.

4. While the stuffing is cooking, in a medium-sized bowl, combine the butter or margarine, wine, oregano, lemon zest, salt, pepper, and garlic. Set aside.

5. Rinse the fish and pat it dry. Then liberally grease a broiler pan, and place the halibut on it. Brush half of the butter mixture over the fish.

6. Place the fish under the broiler, 3 inches below the heat source, and broil for 4 minutes. Turn carefully, brush the second side with the remaining butter mixture, and broil for 4 additional minutes, or just until the flesh changes from translucent to opaque and can be easily flaked with a fork. Halibut cooks quickly, so be careful not to overcook. Serve with the Scampi Stuffing.

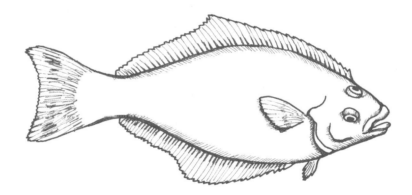

CODANDSHRIMPAUGRATIN

*If you love seafood, you know that two varieties are
better than one! These luscious au gratin cod fillets are
crowned with a savory stuffing of shrimp, tomatoes,
garlic, and seasoned stuffing mix.*

1. Preheat the oven to 375°F. Liberally grease a baking dish and set aside.

2. To make the stuffing, place the oil in a small skillet over medium heat. Add the celery, green onions, and garlic, and sauté for 5 minutes, or until the vegetables are tender but not brown.

3. Place the stuffing mix in a large bowl, and stir in the vegetable mixture. Add the tomato, shrimp, and chicken broth, and toss until well combined.

4. Rinse the fish, pat dry, and arrange on the prepared dish. Spoon the stuffing mixture over the fish fillets and bake uncovered for 20 minutes, or until the fish flakes easily when tested with a fork. Garnish with the lemon slices before serving.

LOBSTERSTUFFING**PIE**

Imagine chunks of delicate lobster cloaked in a rich sauce and surrounded by a crisp, perfectly seasoned crust. Stuffing mix adds just the right blend of flavors to this sublime pie.

1. Preheat the oven to 400°F. Liberally grease a 9-inch pie pan and set aside.

2. To make the crust, place the stuffing mix on a flat surface and use a rolling pin to crush the mix into fine crumbs.

3. Place the stuffing crumbs in a medium-sized bowl and blend in the butter or margarine. Press the mixture firmly against the bottom and sides of the prepared pie pan and set aside.

4. To make the filling, place the butter or margarine and the flour in a medium-sized saucepan and cook over medium heat, blending well. Gradually stir in the milk and cook until thick, stirring constantly. Stir in the lobster, chives, pimiento or red pepper, mustard, salt, and pepper. Remove the saucepan from the heat and fold in the sour cream until blended.

5. Pour the filling into the pie crust and bake for 15 minutes, or until thoroughly heated. Garnish with the parsley before serving.

YIELD: 6 SERVINGS

CRUST

3 cups seasoned stuffing mix

3/4 cup melted butter or margarine

PIE FILLING

1/4 cup melted butter or margarine

1/4 cup all-purpose flour

1 1/2 cups milk

1 pound cooked lobster meat, cut into pieces

3 tablespoons chopped fresh chives

2 tablespoons minced pimiento or red bell pepper

1 teaspoon prepared mustard

Salt to taste

Freshly ground black pepper to taste

1/2 cup sour cream

Parsley for garnish

FILLETOF**SOLE**- WHITE**WINE**ROLL-**UPS**

Who needs a jellyroll for dessert when you have this satisfying roll instead? Fillet of sole is gently sprinkled with a Parmesan cheese filling, rolled, and cooked in white wine for an easy yet elegant entrée.

YIELD: **6 SERVINGS**

6 fillets of sole
(about 5 ounces each)

Salt to taste

Freshly ground black pepper
to taste

I cup dry white wine

FILLING

3 cups cornbread
stuffing mix

2 tablespoons chopped
fresh chives

¼ cup grated
Parmesan cheese

1. Preheat the oven to 350°F. Liberally grease a baking dish and set aside.

2. In a medium-sized bowl, combine all of the filling ingredients.

3. Rinse the fish fillets and pat them dry. Arrange the fillets on a flat surface, and sprinkle the Parmesan mixture over the fish, dividing the mixture evenly. Then roll each fillet up jellyroll style. They will measure about 2 inches high.

4. Arrange the roll-ups seam side down in the prepared dish, and sprinkle with salt and pepper to taste. Pour the wine over the roll-ups, lightly cover with aluminum foil, and bake for 15 minutes. Uncover the fish and cook for 5 additional minutes, or until the fish flakes easily when tested with a fork.

5. **Stuffing**for the**Holidays**

ophie Cubbison didn't need market research to know that Americans look forward to Thanksgiving and Christmas more than any other meals of the year, and that stuffing is their favorite holiday dish. If Sophie had been able to scan national surveys, though, they would have confirmed that in most families, you can skip the turkey or ham, but give stuffing the heave-ho and Christmas will be far less merry. For that reason, Sophie applied her talents to concocting a wide range of wonderfully festive stuffings.

To create this chapter, we pored over decades of archives to select the most tempting recipes that Sophie devised. Holiday stuffings should, of course, be hearty and comforting, yet festive and memorable, and should incorporate seasonal ingredients such as cranberries, apples, and maple syrup. Whether you prepare a refreshing orange stuffing spiked with brandy-soaked currants or a magnificent layered carrot and onion stuffing torte, you'll soon learn that the dishes in this chapter qualify as perfect holiday fare in every respect. Although all of the stuffings in this chapter are baked as casseroles, they can, of course, also be used to stuff a turkey. The inset on page 22 provides tips on making the right amount of stuffing for your bird.

Perhaps best of all, every dish presented in these pages relies on easy-to-use stuffing mix, allowing you to enjoy more time with family and friends. And isn't that what holidays are all about?

CRANBERRY, **MAPLE,** AND **ALMOND** STUFFING

Boasting golden cornbread, tart cranberries, crunchy toasted almonds, and a hint of sweet maple syrup and brown sugar, this festive stuffing will be the talk of your holiday table.

YIELD: 8 SERVINGS

I cup fresh cranberries

$\frac{1}{2}$ cup maple syrup

$\frac{1}{4}$ cup brown sugar

$\frac{1}{2}$ cup butter or margarine

$\frac{1}{2}$ cup chopped onion

$\frac{1}{2}$ cup chopped celery

6 cups cornbread stuffing mix

$\frac{1}{2}$ cup chopped almonds, toasted

$\frac{1}{4}$ cup chicken broth

1. Preheat the oven to 325°F. Lightly grease a 2$\frac{1}{2}$- to 3-quart casserole dish and set aside.

2. Place the cranberries, maple syrup, and brown sugar in a medium-sized saucepan, and cook over low heat, stirring often, for 15 minutes, or just until the cranberries are soft and begin to pop. Set aside.

3. Place the butter or margarine in a large skillet, and melt over medium heat. Add the onion and celery and sauté for 5 minutes, or until the vegetables are soft. Stir in the cranberry mixture, stuffing mix, almonds, and broth, mixing well.

4. Transfer the stuffing to the prepared dish, cover, and bake for 30 to 40 minutes, or until heated through. If a crisp top is desired, uncover the dish and bake for 10 additional minutes.

FESTIVEFIGAND BACONSTUFFING

*This combination of sweet figs, smoky bacon,
and tart apples produces a stunning dish,
worthy of the most special holiday celebrations.*

1. Preheat the oven to 350°F. Lightly grease a 2½- to 3-quart casserole dish and set aside.

2. Place the butter or margarine in a medium-sized skillet, and melt over medium heat. Add the onion and celery and sauté for 5 minutes, or until soft. Stir in the apples, figs, and parsley.

3. Combine the stuffing mix and bacon in a large bowl. Pour the apple mixture over the stuffing mix, add the chicken broth, and stir to combine well.

4. Transfer the stuffing to the prepared dish, cover, and bake for 30 to 40 minutes, or until heated through. If a crisp top is desired, uncover the dish and bake for 10 additional minutes.

YIELD: 8 SERVINGS

¼ cup butter or margarine

I cup chopped onion

I cup chopped celery

3 medium Granny Smith apples, peeled, cored, and chopped

I cup chopped dried figs

½ cup finely chopped fresh parsley

6 cups seasoned or cornbread stuffing mix

4 ounces bacon, diced and cooked crisp

2 cups chicken broth

FRUITEDACORNSQUASH

Acorn squash make lovely holiday centerpieces, but are even more fun as part of the meal! Here, they're baked and filled with cornbread stuffing flavored with apricots, prunes, and almonds.

YIELD: 6 SERVINGS

½ cup melted butter or margarine, divided

2 cups chopped celery

1 cup chopped onion

3 cups seasoned or cornbread stuffing mix

½ cup chopped prunes

½ cup chopped dried apricots

½ cup chopped almonds

1 ½ cups chicken broth

3 small acorn squash (each about 1 pound)

1. Preheat the oven to 350°F. Lightly grease a casserole dish and set aside.

2. Place 2 tablespoons of the butter or margarine in a medium-sized skillet. Add the celery and onion and sauté for about 5 minutes, or until the vegetables are soft.

3. Combine the sautéed vegetables, stuffing mix, and remaining butter or margarine in a large bowl, mixing lightly. Add the prunes, apricots, and almonds, and mix lightly. Stir in as much broth as needed to reach the desired consistency. Set aside.

4. Cut each acorn squash in half crosswise, creating 6 "bowls." If necessary, cut a thick slice from the bottom of each bowl to make the squash stand upright. Using a spoon, scoop out the seeds and stringy portion of the squash, leaving only the flesh and peel. Place the squash upside-down on the prepared casserole dish and bake for 20 minutes, or until they just begin to soften.

5. Remove the dish from the oven, leaving the oven on, and carefully turn the squash over. Fill each with the stuffing, dividing it evenly, and bake for 30 additional minutes, or until the squash are tender and lightly browned on top.

BRANDYANDORANGE STUFFING

If there is any time to break out the brandy, it's during the holiday season. For this stunner of a stuffing, you'll soak currants in the brandy and then add a wee bit more of the flavorful liquor, along with oranges, pears, apricots, and pine nuts.

1. Preheat the oven to 325°F. Lightly grease a 2-quart casserole dish and set aside.

2. Combine the stuffing mix, butter or margarine, and orange zest in a large bowl. Stir in the currants or raisins, along with the brandy they've been soaking in; the orange juice; and the additional tablespoon of brandy. Add all of the remaining ingredients and mix well.

3. Transfer the stuffing to the prepared dish, cover, and bake for 20 to 30 minutes, or until heated through. If a crisp top is desired, uncover the dish and bake for 10 additional minutes.

YIELD: **4 SERVINGS**

3 cups cornbread stuffing mix

$\frac{1}{2}$ cup melted butter or margarine

Zest of one orange, chopped

$\frac{1}{2}$ cup currants or raisins, soaked in 1 tablespoon brandy

$\frac{1}{2}$ cup fresh orange juice

1 tablespoon brandy

$\frac{1}{2}$ cup diced dried apricots

1 small Bartlett pear, unpeeled, cored, and chopped

$\frac{1}{2}$ cup pine nuts, toasted

$\frac{1}{2}$ teaspoon ground cinnamon

$\frac{1}{4}$ teaspoon ground nutmeg

$\frac{1}{4}$ teaspoon ground allspice

Salt to taste

Freshly ground black pepper to taste

WILDRICE, PECAN, AND DRIEDFRUITSTUFFING

With its colorful bouquet of dried fruits,
this wild rice stuffing is an absolute standout.

YIELD: 10 TO 12 SERVINGS

12 ounces loose
pork sausage

4 shallots, quartered

2 1/4 cups low-sodium
chicken broth

1/2 cup wild rice

2 tablespoons plus
1 teaspoon fresh thyme,
minced, divided

3/4 cup long-grain white rice

1/2 cup dried cherries

1/2 cup dried cranberries

1/2 cup golden raisins

3 cups cornbread or
seasoned stuffing mix

1/2 cup chopped pecans,
toasted

1 egg

Salt to taste

Freshly ground pepper
to taste

1. Preheat the oven to 350°F. Liberally grease a 2½- to 3-quart casserole dish and set aside.

2. Place a large skillet over medium-high heat. Add the sausage and cook, breaking the meat up with a fork, until the sausage is brown and no pink remains. Leaving the drippings and sausage in the pan, add the shallots and sauté for an additional 2 minutes. Set aside.

3. Place the chicken broth in a medium-sized saucepan, and bring to a boil over high heat. Add the wild rice and 1 tablespoon of the thyme, and again bring to a boil. Reduce the heat, cover, and simmer for 15 minutes.

4. Add the white rice to the saucepan, cover, and simmer for 10 additional minutes. Stir in the sausage mixture and cook for 5 more minutes, or until the liquid is almost absorbed.

5. Stir the dried cherries, cranberries, and raisins into the rice mixture. Cover and simmer for 2 additional minutes.

6. Remove the saucepan from the heat, and stir in the stuffing mix, pecans, egg, and remaining thyme until combined. Season with salt and pepper to taste.

7. Transfer the stuffing to the prepared dish, cover, and bake for 30 to 40 minutes, or until heated through. If a crisp top is desired, uncover the dish and bake for 10 additional minutes.

YAMAND**RAISIN**STUFFING

Sweet potato casseroles are okay, but you'll turn "okay" into "sensational" when you add cornbread, pineapple juice, chewy raisins, and crunchy pecans.

YIELD: 10 TO 12 SERVINGS

6 cups cornbread stuffing mix

29-ounce can yams, drained and diced

I cup dark raisins

I cup pecan halves

I cup melted butter or margarine

I cup pineapple juice

1. Preheat the oven to 350°F. Lightly grease a 2½- to 3-quart casserole dish and set aside.

2. Combine the stuffing mix, yams, raisins, and pecans in a large bowl, mixing well. Stir in the butter or margarine and the pineapple juice.

3. Transfer the stuffing to the prepared dish, cover, and bake for 30 to 40 minutes, or until heated through. If a crisp top is desired, uncover the dish and bake for 10 additional minutes.

APPLE AND WALNUT STUFFING

This simple apple and walnut stuffing is the epitome of comfort food, and makes a classic addition to any holiday table.

YIELD: 8 SERVINGS

½ cup butter or margarine

1 cup chopped celery

1 cup chopped onion

1 cup chicken broth

¾ cup apple juice

6 cups seasoned stuffing mix

2 cups chopped, peeled Granny Smith apple

1 cup chopped walnuts

1. Preheat the oven to 350°F. Lightly grease a 2½- to 3-quart casserole dish and set aside.

2. Place the butter or margarine in a large skillet, and melt over medium heat. Add the celery and onion and sauté for 5 minutes, or until the vegetables are soft. Add the chicken broth and heat for 2 minutes.

3. In a large bowl, combine all of the remaining ingredients. Add the sautéed vegetable mixture, and mix well.

4. Transfer the stuffing to the prepared dish, cover, and bake for 30 to 40 minutes, or until heated through. If a crisp top is desired, uncover the dish and bake for 10 additional minutes.

PISTACHIO AND APRICOT STUFFING

This stuffing's wonderful blending of flavors—
sweet dates, tart apricots, and mellow pistachios—
will make it a holiday favorite in your home.

YIELD: 4 SERVINGS

1. Preheat the oven to 350°F. Lightly grease a 2-quart casserole dish and set aside.

2. Place the butter or margarine in a large saucepan, and melt over medium heat. Add the onion and sauté for 5 minutes, or until soft.

3. Add the water and apricot or peach nectar to the onion, and cook for 2 additional minutes. Add the stuffing mix and stir until well moistened, adding more water if necessary. Fold in the nuts, apricots, and dates.

4. Transfer the stuffing to the prepared dish, cover, and bake for 20 to 30 minutes, or until heated through. If a crisp top is desired, uncover the dish and bake for 10 additional minutes.

¼ cup butter or margarine

1 cup chopped onion

1 cup water

¾ cup apricot or peach nectar

3 cups seasoned stuffing mix

1 cup chopped pistachio nuts

½ cup diced dried apricots

½ cup chopped dates

CARROTANDONION STUFFINGTORTE

This luscious torte alternates layers of seasoned stuffing and cinnamon-and nutmeg-infused carrots.

YIELD: 8 SERVINGS

1 tablespoon olive oil

$^{1}/_{2}$ cup chopped onion

$^{1}/_{2}$ cup chopped celery

6 cups seasoned or cornbread stuffing mix

1$^{3}/_{4}$ cups apple juice, orange juice, or chicken broth

1 egg, beaten

1 pound carrots (about 6 medium), peeled, cooked, and puréed

2 tablespoons chopped fresh parsley

$^{1}/_{8}$ teaspoon ground cinnamon

$^{1}/_{8}$ teaspoon ground nutmeg

Salt to taste

Freshly ground black pepper to taste

1. Preheat the oven to 375°F. Liberally grease a 9-x-5-inch loaf pan and set aside.

2. Heat the olive oil in a medium-sized skillet over medium heat, and sauté the onion and celery for about 5 minutes, or until soft.

3. Combine the stuffing mix and sautéed vegetables in a large bowl, mixing lightly. Add the juice or broth and the egg, and mix lightly. Set aside.

4. In a separate large bowl, thoroughly combine the carrots, parsley, cinnamon, nutmeg, salt, and pepper. Set aside.

5. Pat half of the stuffing mixture on the bottom of the loaf pan, creating an even layer. Arrange all of the carrot mixture on top of the stuffing, smoothing it out evenly. Top with the remaining stuffing mixture, smoothing it so that the carrot mixture is completely covered.

6. Cover the loaf pan with a sheet of aluminum foil and bake for 25 minutes. Remove the foil and bake for 15 to 20 additional minutes, or just until a crust begins to form on top.

7. Remove the loaf from the oven, and allow to cool for about 10 minutes. Loosen the edges by running a knife between the loaf and the pan, place a serving plate over the pan, and invert, allowing the loaf to slide onto the plate.

BOWL O'**CHERRIES**STUFFING

The addition of cherries to this otherwise savory stuffing lends the dish a tart sweetness and a festive splash of color.

1. Preheat the oven to 350°F. Liberally grease a 2-quart casserole dish and set aside.

2. Place the butter or margarine in a medium-sized saucepan, and melt over medium heat. Add the celery and onion and sauté for 5 minutes, or until the vegetables are soft. Stir in the thyme and poultry seasoning.

3. In a large bowl, toss together the stuffing mix, sautéed vegetables, and broth. Gently stir in the cherries.

4. Transfer the stuffing to the prepared dish, cover, and bake for 20 to 30 minutes, or until heated through. If a crisp top is desired, uncover the dish and bake for 10 additional minutes.

YIELD: 4 SERVINGS

2 tablespoons butter or margarine

3/4 cup chopped celery

1/2 cup chopped onion

1 teaspoon dried thyme

1/4 teaspoon poultry seasoning

3 cups seasoned stuffing mix

3/4 cup chicken broth

2 cups frozen pitted cherries, thawed and drained, or 2 cups canned pitted cherries, drained

SHERRIEDCORNBREAD STUFFING

*Sherry adds an elegant touch to this hearty cornbread stuffing,
which is flecked with fresh parsley.*

YIELD: 8 SERVINGS

½ cup butter or margarine

I cup chopped celery

½ cup chopped onion

10.75-ounce can condensed cream of chicken soup

¾ cup dry sherry

6 cups cornbread stuffing mix

½ cup chopped fresh parsley

1. Preheat the oven to 350°F. Lightly grease a 2½- to 3-quart casserole dish and set aside.

2. Place the butter or margarine in a medium-sized skillet, and melt over medium heat. Add the celery and onion and sauté for 5 minutes, or until the vegetables are soft. Set aside.

3. Place the soup and sherry in a small bowl, and stir to combine. Set aside.

4. Combine the stuffing mix, sautéed vegetables, and parsley in a large bowl. Pour the soup mixture over the stuffing, and stir until well combined.

5. Transfer the stuffing to the prepared dish, cover, and bake for 30 to 40 minutes, or until heated through. If a crisp top is desired, uncover the dish and bake for 10 additional minutes.

6. **Regional**and International**Stuffings**

Sophie Cubbison was an avid traveler. But as she crisscrossed the globe, the sights she found most inspiring weren't those of the Statue of Liberty or Big Ben. Rather, Sophie was fascinated by the sights of both professional and home chefs preparing stuffings with native ingredients, and her souvenirs were often ideas for recreating the flavors of her travels.

This chapter is the result of Sophie's delicious forays into the cuisines of many different regions and countries. In the following pages, you will find a spicy Southwestern stuffing enlivened with chorizo sausage and salsa; a Chinese creation that unites ground pork, fresh ginger, sesame seeds, and water chestnuts; and much much more. And thanks to the use of stuffing mix, every stuffing is not only mouth-watering, but also amazingly fast and easy to make.

Although the following stuffings are baked as casseroles, they can also be used to stuff a turkey. If you want to fill your bird with, say, Taste of Italy Stuffing, see the inset on page 22 for tips on making the right amount of stuffing.

Whether you want to sample the traditional oyster stuffing of New England or the red mole stuffing inspired by Mexican cuisine, we hope you'll consider these recipes a tasty travelogue. Enjoy the trip!

NEW**ENGLAND**OYSTER
DRESSING

*Oysters were so plentiful in Colonial New England that they were
not only eaten by the colonists, but also fed to the livestock!
Nowadays, of course, oysters are considered a delicacy and
reserved for special recipes such as this delicious oyster dressing.*

YIELD: 8 SERVINGS

I cup butter or margarine

2 cups diced celery

I ½ cups finely
chopped onion

⅓ cup finely chopped
fresh parsley

½ teaspoon freshly ground
black pepper

6 cups seasoned or
cornbread stuffing mix

I pound fresh-shucked
oysters, or 2 (8-ounce) jars
whole oysters, drained

½ cup oyster liquor or
chicken broth

1. Preheat the oven to 325°F. Lightly grease a 2½- to 3-quart casserole dish and set aside.

2. Place the butter or margarine in a large saucepan, and melt over medium heat. Add the celery and onion and sauté for 5 minutes, or until the vegetables are soft. Do not allow to brown.

3. Add the parsley and pepper to the saucepan. Then stir in the stuffing mix, followed by the oysters. (Chop the oysters prior to adding them if you prefer chopped to whole.) Add just enough oyster liquor or broth to reach the desired consistency.

4. Transfer the stuffing to the prepared dish, cover, and bake for 30 to 40 minutes, or until the stuffing is heated through and the oysters are fully cooked. If a crisp top is desired, uncover the dish and bake for 10 additional minutes.

SPICY**SOUTHWESTERN** CORN**STUFFING**

Spend even a day traveling in the beautiful Southwest and most likely you will eat chilies and corn a few times over. That's why these ingredients make the perfect touches for this mildly spicy cornbread stuffing.

1. Preheat the oven to 350°F. Lightly grease a 2-quart casserole dish and set aside.

2. Combine all of the ingredients, except the melted butter or margarine, in a large bowl, tossing them together until well mixed. If a moister stuffing is desired, add melted butter or margarine.

3. Transfer the stuffing to the prepared dish, cover, and bake for 20 to 30 minutes, or until heated through. If a crisp top is desired, uncover the dish and bake for 10 additional minutes.

YIELD: 4 SERVINGS

3 cups cornbread stuffing mix

14.75-ounce can creamed corn

1/2 cup canned diced green chilies, drained

1/4 cup chopped onion

1 egg, lightly beaten

1 1/2 teaspoons salt

1/8 teaspoon freshly ground black pepper

Melted butter or margarine as needed

TEXAS-**STYLE**BOURBON **STUFFING**

*This Texas-style stuffing gets its kick from bourbon
and chili powder. If a spicier dish is desired,
increase the amount of chili powder.*

YIELD: 8 SERVINGS

¹/₄ cup butter or margarine,
softened

I cup chopped celery

³/₄ cup finely chopped onion

¹/₂ cup finely chopped
green bell pepper

6 cups cornbread
stuffing mix

¹/₂ cup chopped
fresh parsley

¹/₂ teaspoon chili powder
or to taste

3 eggs

¹/₄ cup bourbon

I teaspoon fresh
lemon juice

1. Preheat the oven to 325°F. Lightly grease a 2¹/₂- to 3-quart casserole dish and set aside.

2. Place the butter or margarine in a medium-sized skillet, and melt over medium heat. Add the celery, onion, and green pepper and sauté for 5 minutes, or until the vegetables are soft.

3. Combine the stuffing mix, sautéed vegetables, parsley, and chili powder in a large bowl. Set aside.

4. Place the eggs, bourbon, and lemon juice in a small bowl and beat to combine. Pour over the stuffing mixture and toss to blend.

5. Transfer the stuffing to the prepared dish, cover, and bake for 30 to 40 minutes, or until heated through. If a crisp top is desired, uncover the dish and bake for 10 additional minutes.

HAWAIIANTROPICALSTUFFING

*This wonderful stuffing will leave guests satisfied well after
everyone has said "aloha." The sweetness of pineapple and
coconut milk is balanced by the punch of onions and cilantro.
Macadamia nuts add a much-appreciated crunch.*

YIELD: **4** SERVINGS

$^1/_2$ cup butter or margarine

$^1/_2$ cup chopped celery

$^1/_2$ cup chopped onion

$^1/_2$ cup canned pineapple
chunks, undrained

$^1/_4$ cup minced fresh
cilantro

$^1/_2$ cup coconut milk

3 cups seasoned
stuffing mix

$^1/_2$ cup chopped
macadamia nuts

$^1/_2$ cup shredded coconut

I egg, lightly beaten

1. Preheat the oven to 325°F. Lightly grease a 2-quart casserole
dish and set aside.

2. Place the butter or margarine in a large skillet, and melt
over medium heat. Add the celery, onion, pineapple, and
cilantro, and sauté for about 5 minutes, or until the vegetables are soft.

3. Stir the coconut milk into the skillet mixture. Then stir in the
stuffing mix, macadamia nuts, shredded coconut, and egg.

4. Transfer the stuffing to the prepared dish, cover, and bake
for 20 to 30 minutes, or until heated through. If a crisp top is
desired, uncover the dish and bake for 10 additional minutes.

TASTE OF ITALY STUFFING

If your family loves the distinctive flavors of Italy, this stuffing—featuring Parmesan, marinated artichokes, and Italian spices—will be a sure-fire winner.

YIELD: 8 SERVINGS

2 (6-ounce) jars marinated artichoke hearts, undrained, coarsely chopped

6 cups seasoned stuffing mix

10-ounce package frozen chopped spinach, thawed and squeezed dry

1/2 cup grated Parmesan or Romano cheese

1 teaspoon dried oregano

1 teaspoon dried basil

1 cup dry white wine, dry sherry, or broth

1. Preheat the oven to 325°F. Liberally grease a 2½- to 3-quart casserole dish and set aside.

2. Combine the artichokes, along with the marinating liquid, and the stuffing in a large bowl. Add all of the remaining ingredients except for the wine or broth, and toss together lightly. Add the wine and mix, adding more liquid if a moister stuffing is desired.

3. Transfer the stuffing to the prepared dish, cover, and bake for 30 to 40 minutes, or until heated through. If a crisp top is desired, uncover the dish and bake for 10 additional minutes.

MEDITERRANEAN
STUFFING

*Sun-drenched olives and sun-dried tomatoes highlight this
Mediterranean stuffing, which is also kissed by red wine.*

YIELD: 8 SERVINGS

6 cups seasoned
stuffing mix

I cup chopped onion

I cup chopped black olives

½ cup olive oil

6-ounce jar marinated
artichoke hearts, undrained,
finely chopped

½ cup chopped marinated
sun-dried tomatoes,
drained

½ cup red wine or water

½ cup chicken broth

1. Preheat the oven to 325°F. Lightly grease a 2½- to 3-quart casserole dish and set aside.

2. Combine all of the ingredients in a large bowl, mixing thoroughly.

3. Transfer the stuffing to the prepared dish, cover, and bake for 30 to 40 minutes, or until heated through. If a crisp top is desired, uncover the dish and bake for 10 additional minutes.

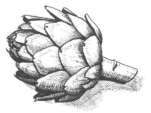

CHINESE-**GINGER**-SESAME **STUFFING**

Master Chef Martin Yan, host of the long-running PBS TV show
Yan Can Cook *and one of our beloved collaborators,*
created this delicious Asian-inspired stuffing.

YIELD: 8 SERVINGS

4 ounces ground pork

2 teaspoons soy sauce

4 teaspoons dry sherry, divided

2 teaspoons vegetable oil

1 teaspoon minced garlic

1 teaspoon minced fresh ginger

1 cup sliced green onions

1 cup sliced water chestnuts

1 ½ cups chicken broth or water

3 tablespoons hoisin sauce

¾ teaspoon sesame oil

6 cups seasoned stuffing mix

1. Preheat the oven to 325°F. Lightly grease a 2½- to 3-quart casserole dish and set aside.

2. Place the ground pork in a small bowl and mix in the soy sauce and 1 teaspoon of the sherry. Set aside for 15 minutes.

3. Heat a wok or large skillet over high heat. Add the oil, swirling to coat the sides. Add the garlic and ginger and cook for about 5 seconds. Add the pork and stir-fry for 2 minutes, or until the pork is no longer pink. Add the green onions and stir-fry for 1 minute. Add the water chestnuts and stir-fry for 30 seconds. Remove from the heat.

4. Combine the remaining 3 teaspoons of sherry and the broth or water, hoisin sauce, and sesame oil in a small bowl. Add it to the contents of the wok, and stir to combine. Then add the stuffing mix, tossing gently until well moistened.

5. Transfer the stuffing to the prepared dish, cover, and bake for 30 to 40 minutes, or until heated through. If a crisp top is desired, uncover the dish and bake for 10 additional minutes.

CHINESE SHIITAKE MUSHROOM STUFFING

This is another favorite stuffing recipe created by TV star and prolific cookbook author Martin Yan. Its authentic flavor comes from Chinese sausage, minced ginger, shiitake mushrooms, and oyster sauce.

1. Preheat the oven to 325°F. Lightly grease a 2½- to 3-quart casserole dish and set aside.

2. Heat a wok or large skillet over high heat. Carefully add the vegetable oil, swirling to coat the sides. Add the Chinese sausage or bacon and the ginger, and stir-fry until fragrant, about 30 seconds. Add the carrots, water chestnuts, mushrooms, and green onions, and stir-fry for 2 minutes. Remove the wok from the heat.

3. Add the stuffing mix, oyster sauce, sesame oil, and pepper to the wok, and stir to combine. Stir in just enough water or broth to moisten.

4. Transfer the stuffing to the prepared dish, cover, and bake for 30 to 40 minutes, or until heated through. If a crisp top is desired, uncover the dish and bake for 10 additional minutes.

YIELD: **8 SERVINGS**

2 tablespoons vegetable oil

I Chinese sausage,* thinly sliced, or ½ cup cooked and crumbled bacon (about 8 ounces uncooked)

I tablespoon minced fresh ginger

⅓ cup thinly sliced carrots

⅓ cup sliced water chestnuts

½ cup sliced fresh shiitake mushrooms

4 green onions, sliced

6 cups seasoned stuffing mix

3 tablespoons oyster sauce

2 teaspoons sesame oil

½ teaspoon freshly ground white pepper

1 ½ to 2 cups water or chicken broth

---

* Chinese sausage is available in many Asian markets.

MEXICANRED MOLESTUFFING

This stuffing owes its South-of-the-Border flavor to red mole paste—a fragrant paste made by combining ground unsweetened chocolate with herbs and ground chilies. Look for it in specialty stores and Mexican markets.

YIELD: 8 SERVINGS

1/4 cup butter or margarine

1 1/2 cups diced chayote*
or zucchini

3/4 cup diced red onion

1/2 cup diced celery

1 clove garlic, minced

6 cups seasoned
stuffing mix

2 cups chicken broth

2 tablespoons
red mole paste

---

* Chayote—a member of the squash family—is available in some supermarkets, specialty stores, and Mexican markets.

1. Preheat the oven to 325°F. Lightly grease a 2 1/2- to 3-quart casserole dish and set aside.

2. Place the butter or margarine in a large skillet, and melt over medium heat. Add the chayote or zucchini, onion, celery, and garlic, and sauté for 5 minutes, or until the vegetables are tender. Stir in the stuffing mix and remove the skillet from the heat, setting it aside.

3. Place the broth in a medium-sized saucepan and bring to a boil over high heat. Reduce the heat to low, add the mole paste, and use a wire whisk to whip the broth for 10 minutes, or until well mixed.

4. Stir 1 cup of the mole sauce into the stuffing mixture. Then transfer the stuffing to the prepared dish, cover, and bake for 30 to 40 minutes, or until heated through. If a crisp top is desired, uncover the dish and bake for 10 additional minutes. Reheat the remaining mole sauce and serve alongside the stuffing, or use it to baste poultry or meat.

MEXICAN**CHORIZO**AND **SALSA**STUFFING

Chorizo—a pork sausage flavored with garlic, chili powder, and other spices—kicks up the heat in this Mexican-inspired stuffing, which also gets its flavor from spicy tomato juice, green chile salsa, and olives.

1. Preheat the oven to 350°F. Lightly grease a 2½- to 3-quart casserole dish and set aside.

2. Place a medium-sized skillet over medium heat. Add the sausage and cook, breaking the meat up with a fork, until the sausage is brown and no pink remains. Remove the sausage from any fat that has accumulated, and blot any remaining fat from the sausage with paper towels.

3. In a large bowl, combine the sausage with all of the remaining ingredients except for the tomato juice and butter or margarine. Stir in the juice and butter.

4. Transfer the stuffing to the prepared dish, cover, and bake for 30 to 40 minutes, or until heated through. If a crisp top is desired, uncover the dish and bake for 10 additional minutes.

YIELD: 8 SERVINGS

8 ounces chorizo or other spicy sausage, casings removed

6 cups cornbread stuffing mix

I cup chopped black olives

I cup chopped celery

I cup fresh or canned whole kernel corn, drained

½ cup green chile salsa

I cup spicy tomato juice

¾ cup melted butter or margarine

GERMAN-STYLE APPLE AND SAUSAGE STUFFING

Comfort food may have been born in Germany, where rich dishes like this sausage-and-apple stuffing are well loved.

YIELD: 8 SERVINGS

1 pound bratwurst, sliced

6 cups seasoned stuffing mix

2 Granny Smith apples, peeled, cored, and diced

1 cup chopped celery

1/2 cup chopped onion

1 1/2 cups water or chicken broth

1. Preheat the oven to 325°F. Liberally grease a 2½- to 3-quart casserole dish and set aside.

2. Place a large skillet over medium heat. Add the sausage and cook until browned.

3. In a large bowl, combine the cooked sausage, as well as the sausage drippings, with all of the remaining ingredients except for the water or chicken broth. Stir in the liquid.

4. Transfer the stuffing to the prepared dish, cover, and bake for 30 to 40 minutes, or until heated through. If a crisp top is desired, uncover the dish and bake for 10 additional minutes.

7. Low-**Fat,** Fruit, **and** Vegetable**Stuffings**

National polls show that many people view stuffing as an indulgent treat that should be enjoyed only once in a while. But while certainly a treat, a good stuffing doesn't have to be "saved" for the holidays. Every recipe in this book demonstrates how stuffing mixes make it possible to enjoy a sensational side dish even during a busy work week. And this chapter will show you how simple it is to make stuffings that are low enough in fat and high enough in nutrients to be enjoyed with any meal—not just on special occasions.

Long before there were a dozen health food stores in the country, there was Cubbison's Health Food Store. Because of Sophie's interest in natural foods, it's not surprising that she often chose to combine her stuffing mix with nuts, fresh and dried fruits, and vegetables. We are delighted to bring some of her most enticing healthful creations into your kitchen with offerings such as Apple, Sunflower, and Watercress Stuffing; Crunchy Mushroom Stuffing; Four Onion Stuffing; Spicy Artichoke Stuffing; and Sun-Dried Tomato Stuffing. Although all of the stuffings in this chapter are baked as casseroles, they can, of course, also be used to stuff a turkey. See the inset on page 22 for tips on making the right amount of stuffing for your bird.

Should stuffing be relegated to the winter holidays or a once-in-a-blue-moon special occasion? Once you've sampled a few of the following dishes, we think you'll agree that it's possible to have your stuffing and eat it, too!

APPLESAUCECORNBREAD STUFFING

Applesauce is a sweet, innovative way to add moisture to this delicious cornbread stuffing without the use of butter, margarine, or oil. Ground cinnamon gives the dish its very special flavor.

YIELD: **8 SERVINGS**

3 cups applesauce

I teaspoon ground cinnamon

6 cups cornbread stuffing mix

I cup apple juice

1. Preheat the oven to 325°F. Coat a 2½- to 3-quart casserole dish with nonstick cooking spray and set aside.

2. Combine the applesauce and cinnamon in a large bowl. Add the stuffing mix, stirring well to combine. Add only enough apple juice to moisten the mixture.

3. Transfer the stuffing to the prepared dish, cover, and bake for 30 to 40 minutes, or until heated through. If a crisp top is desired, uncover the dish and bake for 10 additional minutes.

CRANBERRYSTUFFING

*Nothing is missing from this outstanding cranberry stuffing
except for the fat usually contributed by butter, margarine,
or oil. In this case, chicken broth and egg whites
moisten the stuffing and bind it together.*

YIELD: 8 SERVINGS

2 cups reduced-sodium
chicken broth, divided

1 cup chopped celery

1/2 cup chopped onion

6 cups seasoned or cornbread
stuffing mix

3/4 cup chopped dried
cranberries

3 egg whites

1 1/2 tablespoons chopped
fresh parsley

1 1/2 teaspoons poultry
seasoning

1/2 teaspoon salt

1. Preheat the oven to 325°F. Coat a 2½- to 3-quart casserole dish with nonstick cooking spray and set aside.

2. Place ½ cup of the chicken broth in a medium skillet, and place over low-medium heat. Add the celery and onion and sauté for 5 minutes, or until the vegetables are tender.

3. Combine the sautéed vegetables with the stuffing mix, cranberries, egg whites, parsley, poultry seasoning, and salt in a large bowl. Stir in the remaining 1½ cups of chicken broth.

4. Transfer the stuffing to the prepared dish, cover, and bake for 30 to 40 minutes, or until heated through. If a crisp top is desired, uncover the dish and bake for 10 additional minutes.

CARROTAND**RAISIN**STUFFING

The sweetness and substance of carrots, raisins, pineapple,
apple juice, and applesauce ensure that you will be
filled up rather than out by this luscious stuffing.

YIELD: 8 SERVINGS

6 cups cornbread stuffing

3 cups applesauce

1 cup chopped carrots

1 cup dark raisins

1 cup canned crushed
pineapple (preferably packed
in natural juices), undrained

½ cup apple juice

½ cup water

1. Preheat the oven to 325°F. Coat a 2½- to 3-quart casserole dish with nonstick cooking spray and set aside.

2. Combine all of the ingredients, except for the apple juice and water, in a large bowl. Stir in the apple juice and water.

3. Transfer the stuffing to the prepared dish, cover, and bake for 30 to 40 minutes, or until heated through. If a crisp top is desired, uncover the dish and bake for 10 additional minutes.

WHEAT**GERM**'N' **HONEY**STUFFING

Wheat germ and honey lend this fruit-filled stuffing
a distinctive nutty yet sweet taste.

1. Preheat the oven to 325°F. Coat a 2½- to 3-quart casserole dish with nonstick cooking spray and set aside.

2. Combine all of the ingredients except for the apple juice in a large bowl, stirring well. Stir in the juice.

3. Transfer the stuffing to the prepared dish, cover, and bake for 30 to 40 minutes, or until heated through. If a crisp top is desired, uncover the dish and bake for 10 additional minutes.

YIELD: 8 SERVINGS

6 cups cornbread stuffing mix

2 egg whites

½ cup wheat germ

½ cup chopped dried apricots

½ cup golden raisins

½ cup honey

¼ teaspoon salt

Zest of 1 lemon

1 ¼ cups apple juice

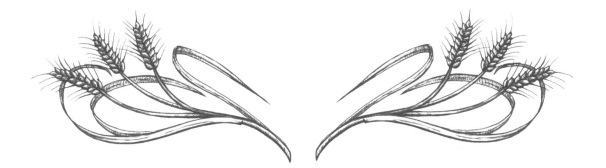

APPLE, SUNFLOWER SEED, AND WATERCRESS STUFFING

*This stuffing packs a sizeable health punch, combining fruits,
vegetables, nuts, seeds, and grains. The flavor is a delicate
mixture of sweet and savory with a crunchy texture
that's out of this world.*

YIELD: 8 SERVINGS

6 cups seasoned or
cornbread stuffing mix

2 apples, unpeeled and diced

½ cup chopped watercress

½ cup slivered almonds

½ cup hulled sunflower seeds

½ cup wheat germ

¼ cup melted butter
or margarine

1 cup pineapple juice

¾ cup water

1. Preheat the oven to 325°F. Coat a 2½- to 3-quart casserole dish with nonstick cooking spray and set aside.

2. In a large bowl, combine all of the ingredients except for the butter and margarine, pineapple juice, and water. Stir in the butter, juice, and water.

3. Transfer the stuffing to the prepared dish, cover, and bake for 30 to 40 minutes, or until heated through. If a crisp top is desired, uncover the dish and bake for 10 additional minutes.

TRIPLECITRUSSTUFFING

*Is there a more delicious way to get your vitamin C than with
this outstanding orange, grapefruit, and tangerine stuffing?
One taste of this triple-citrus treat and you'll be sold!*

1. Preheat the oven to 325°F. Coat a 2-quart casserole dish with
   nonstick cooking spray and set aside.

2. Combine the stuffing mix with the grapefruit, orange, and
   tangerine pieces in a large bowl. Stir in the walnuts, celery,
   and parsley. Stir in first the butter or margarine, and then
   the orange juice and water.

3. Transfer the stuffing to the prepared dish, cover, and bake
   for 20 to 30 minutes, or until heated through. If a crisp top is
   desired, uncover the dish and bake for 10 additional minutes.

YIELD: 4 SERVINGS

3 cups cornbread stuffing mix

¾ cup coarsely chopped
grapefruit segments

½ cup coarsely chopped
orange segments

¼ cup coarsely chopped
tangerine segments

¼ cup chopped walnuts

¼ cup chopped celery

2 tablespoons chopped
fresh parsley

2 tablespoons melted butter
or margarine

¾ cup orange juice

¼ cup water

SAUTEEDAPRICOTSTUFFING

The rich flavor of this stuffing is deepened by sautéing the apricots in butter. Crunchy pecans provide the perfect accent.

YIELD: 8 SERVINGS

1/4 cup butter or margarine

I cup chopped celery

I cup chopped onion

3/4 cup chopped dried apricots

I cup chicken broth

6 cups cornbread stuffing mix

1/2 cup chopped pecans

3/4 cup orange juice

1. Preheat the oven to 325°F. Coat a 2½- to 3-quart casserole dish with nonstick cooking spray and set aside.

2. Place the butter or margarine in a large skillet, and melt over medium heat. Add the celery, onion, and apricots and sauté for about 5 minutes, or until the vegetables are tender. Add the chicken broth and heat for 2 minutes. Set aside.

3. Combine the stuffing mix and pecans in a large bowl. Stir in the apricot mixture and the orange juice, mixing well.

4. Transfer the stuffing to the prepared dish, cover, and bake for 30 to 40 minutes, or until heated through. If a crisp top is desired, uncover the dish and bake for 10 additional minutes.

DRIEDFRUIT
COMPOTE**STUFFING**

*This recipe was inspired by Sophie's fruitcake, which she would
give to family and friends around holiday time. Bursting
with apricots, figs, prunes, and raisins, it is sure to
remind you of your own favorite fruitcake.*

YIELD: 8 SERVINGS

6 cups cornbread
stuffing mix

³/₄ cup chopped prunes

¹/₂ cup chopped dried
apricots

¹/₂ cup chopped dried figs

¹/₄ cup dark raisins

1 ³/₄ cups water

¹/₄ cup melted butter
or margarine

1 tablespoon lemon juice

1. Preheat the oven to 325°F. Coat a 2¹/₂- to 3-quart casserole
dish with nonstick cooking spray and set aside.

2. Combine the stuffing mix and all the dried fruits in a large
bowl, tossing to mix. Stir in the water, butter or margarine,
and lemon juice, mixing well.

3. Transfer the stuffing to the prepared dish, cover, and bake
for 30 to 40 minutes, or until heated through. If a crisp top is
desired, uncover the dish and bake for 10 additional minutes.

SPICYARTICHOKE
STUFFING

If you like artichokes, you'll love this stuffing—a flavorful
blend of cornbread, marinated artichokes, white wine,
and Parmesan, with just a touch of aromatic cumin.

YIELD: 4 SERVINGS

3 cups cornbread
stuffing mix

6-ounce jar marinated
artichoke hearts,
chopped, undrained

2 tablespoons melted
butter or margarine

1/4 cup chopped celery

1/4 cup chopped onion

1 clove garlic, minced

1/8 teaspoon ground cumin

1/2 cup dry white wine

1/2 cup water

1/4 cup grated
Parmesan cheese

1. Preheat the oven to 325°F. Coat a 2-quart casserole dish with nonstick cooking spray and set aside.

2. Combine the stuffing mix, artichokes, butter or margarine, celery, onion, garlic, and cumin in a large bowl. Stir in the wine and water.

3. Transfer the stuffing to the prepared dish and sprinkle with the Parmesan cheese. Cover and bake for 20 to 30 minutes, or until heated through. If a crisp top is desired, uncover the dish and bake for 10 additional minutes.

CRUNCHYMUSHROOM **STUFFING**

Tender mushrooms and crunchy water chestnuts complement each other perfectly in this savory stuffing.

YIELD: 8 SERVINGS

1/4 cup butter or margarine

3 cups chopped fresh mushrooms

1/2 cup chopped onion

1 3/4 cups chicken broth

6 cups seasoned stuffing mix

3/4 cup chopped water chestnuts, drained

1. Preheat the oven to 325°F. Coat a 2½- to 3-quart casserole dish with nonstick cooking spray and set aside.

2. Place the butter or margarine in a large skillet, and melt over low-medium heat. Add the mushrooms and onion and sauté for 5 minutes, or until the vegetables are soft. Stir in the chicken broth and cook for 2 additional minutes. Set aside.

3. Combine the stuffing mix and water chestnuts in a large bowl, mixing well. Stir in the mushroom mixture.

4. Transfer the stuffing to the prepared dish, cover, and bake for 30 to 40 minutes, or until heated through. If a crisp top is desired, uncover the dish and bake for 10 additional minutes.

FOURONION**STUFFING**

Perfect for the onion lover in your house, this wonderful stuffing combines white, red, and green onions with leeks. Onion's sultry cousin garlic is a tasty addition.

YIELD: 8 SERVINGS

¼ cup butter or margarine

¼ cup chopped white onion

¼ cup chopped red onion

2 green onions, white part and 1-inch green part, thinly sliced

2 medium leeks, white part only, finely chopped

1 clove garlic, minced

¼ cup chopped celery

6 cups seasoned stuffing mix

1 cup chopped pecans, toasted

2 tablespoons chopped fresh parsley

1 ½ cups chicken broth

1. Preheat the oven to 325°F. Coat a 2½- to 3-quart casserole dish with nonstick cooking spray and set aside.

2. Place the butter or margarine in a large skillet, and melt over medium heat. Add the white and red onions, green onions, leeks, and garlic, and sauté for 5 minutes, or until golden. Add the celery and cook for 5 additional minutes, or until the celery is tender.

3. Combine the onion mixture, stuffing mix, pecans, and parsley in a large bowl, mixing well. Stir in just enough chicken broth to moisten, mixing lightly.

4. Transfer the stuffing to the prepared dish, cover, and bake for 30 to 40 minutes, or until heated through. If a crisp top is desired, uncover the dish and bake for 10 additional minutes.

SUN-DRIED**TOMATO**AND PINENUT**STUFFING**

*A blending of sophisticated flavors, this luscious stuffing
is nevertheless a snap to prepare.*

YIELD: 8 SERVINGS

1. Preheat the oven to 325°F. Coat a 2½- to 3-quart casserole dish with nonstick cooking spray and set aside.

2. Place the grape or apple juice, wine, and sun-dried tomatoes in a medium-sized saucepan, and bring to a boil. Remove the pan from the heat and allow to sit for about 5 minutes, or until the tomatoes are soft and tender. Drain off and reserve the liquid, allowing it to cool. Finely chop the tomatoes.

3. Combine the tomatoes, stuffing mix, onion, celery, and pine nuts in a large bowl. Mix in the butter or margarine and the reserved liquid, adding more grape juice if needed to reach the desired consistency.

4. Transfer the stuffing to the prepared dish, cover, and bake for 30 to 40 minutes, or until heated through. If a crisp top is desired, uncover the dish and bake for 10 additional minutes.

1 cup white grape juice
or apple juice

¾ cup Madeira or
port wine

½ cup sun-dried tomatoes
(not packed in oil)

6 cups seasoned
stuffing mix

¾ cup chopped onion

¾ cup chopped celery

½ cup pine nuts, toasted

¼ cup melted butter
or margarine

Toasting Nuts

Although nuts can be added to stuffings right out of the package, toasting them intensifies their flavor, further enhancing the dish. Fortunately, nuts can be toasted quickly and easily.

If you choose to toast the nuts in the oven, simply arrange them in a single layer on a baking sheet and bake at 325°F for about 10 minutes, or until lightly browned with a toasted smell. Be sure to check the nuts often, as they can quickly burn, and to stir them every few minutes. Also keep in mind that chopped, sliced, and slivered nuts will toast more quickly than whole nuts.

It's also a snap to toast nuts on the top of the stove. Place the nuts in a skillet over medium-low heat, and cook, stirring often, until lightly browned. Again, you'll want to watch the pan closely as nuts can quickly turn from pale to black.

If desired, toast large batch of nuts and store for a variety of uses—other stuffings, salads, and baking, for instance. Placed in an airtight container, the nuts will stay fresh in the refrigerator for several weeks.

8.ShapingUp Stuffing

Although Sophie Cubbison may have begun by whipping up bowls of savory stuffings for poultry, meat, and fish, it didn't take her long to recognize the versatility of stuffing mix. Soon, she was creating tempting stuffing loaves, muffins, balls, fritters, puffs, cakes, croquettes, and other delicacies. This not only meant that stuffing didn't have to take the usual form of a mounded side dish on a dinner plate, but also that stuffing could escape the bounds of dinner altogether and delight the family at other meals of the day, or even appear as a welcome change at snack time!

For this chapter, we've rounded up some of Sophie's all-time best "shaped" stuffing recipes to enliven your next meal, or to bring oohs and aahs at your next potluck supper. In the following pages, you will find Savory Cranberry Stuffing Loaf, Pumpkin Stuffing Balls, Broccoli and Cheddar Stuffing Croquettes, Creamed Corn Fritters, and even delicate Stuffing Soufflés. These are dishes for every taste and every occasion. Perhaps best of all, although many dishes would make festive additions to your holiday table, each and every one is quick and easy to fix so that you can enjoy your favorite shaped stuffing dish even on a hectic weeknight.

Is there anything wrong with serving a simple stuffing casserole? Of course not! But with Mrs. Cubbison's help, you can surprise family and friends with a variety of enticing creations, each one sure to be a winner.

FIGAND**ORANGE** **STUFFING**LOAF

*Figs and oranges add wonderful flavor
to this sweet and savory loaf.*

1. Preheat the oven to 350°F. Grease eight mini ($4\frac{1}{2}$-x-$2\frac{1}{2}$-x-$1\frac{1}{2}$-inch) loaf pans, or one 9-x-5-inch loaf pan. Set aside.

2. Combine the stuffing mix, celery, orange, and figs in a large bowl, mixing well. Stir in the eggs, butter or margarine, and milk.

3. Divide the mixture evenly among the prepared loaf pans, packing the mixture into the pans.

4. Bake uncovered for 35 minutes for the mini loaves or 50 minutes for the large loaf, or until the stuffing is firm to the touch.

5. Allow the loaves to rest in the pans for about 10 minutes. Then run a knife around the edges to loosen the loaves, unmold, and serve.

SAVORY**CRANBERRY** **STUFFING**LOAF

*Cookbook author Marcie Rothman is one of the talented chefs who
carried on Sophie Cubbison's legacy. This delicious loaf,
flavored with fresh cranberries and orange juice,
is one of Marcie's all-time favorite creations.*

YIELD: 8 SERVINGS

$\frac{1}{4}$ cup melted butter,
margarine, or vegetable oil

3 stalks celery,
finely chopped

I medium onion,
finely chopped

I $\frac{3}{4}$ cups orange juice,
broth, or water

$\frac{2}{3}$ cup fresh cranberries,
coarsely chopped

6 cups cornbread
stuffing mix

1. Preheat the oven to 350°F. Grease a 9-x-5-inch loaf pan and set aside.

2. Heat the butter, margarine, or oil in a large skillet over medium-high heat. Add the celery and onion and cook for 1 minute. Add the juice, broth, or water and the cranberries, and bring to a boil. Cover the skillet, reduce the heat, and simmer for 3 minutes.

3. Remove the skillet from the heat and stir in the stuffing, mixing well. Pack the mixture into the prepared loaf pan.

4. Cover the pan with aluminum foil and bake for 30 minutes, or until thoroughly heated. If a crisp top is desired, uncover the pan and bake for 5 to 10 additional minutes.

5. Allow the loaf to rest in the pan for about 10 minutes. Then run a knife around the edges to loosen the loaf, unmold, and serve.

STUFFINS

If you have never tasted stuffins—stuffing muffins—
you're in for a treat. This basic recipe flavors a cornbread-
stuffing base with fresh onion and parsley.

YIELD: **12** SERVINGS

I cup all-purpose flour

1 ½ tablespoons
baking powder

¾ teaspoon poultry
seasoning

¼ teaspoon salt

2 cups cornbread
stuffing mix

½ cup minced onion

3 tablespoons chopped
fresh parsley

3 eggs

1 ⅓ cups chicken broth

⅓ cup vegetable oil

1. Preheat the oven to 425°F. Liberally grease 12 muffin cups to the rims and set aside.

2. Place the flour, baking powder, poultry seasoning, and salt in a medium-sized bowl, and stir together. Stir in the stuffing mix, onion, and parsley.

3. Place the eggs in a small bowl and beat. Add the chicken broth and oil, and blend well. Stir the egg mixture into the stuffing mixture just until moistened.

4. Spoon the batter into the muffin cups, dividing it evenly among the cups. Bake uncovered for 20 minutes or until golden brown.

5. Allow the muffins to rest in the cups for 5 minutes. Then run a knife around the rims to loosen the muffins, unmold, and serve.

APPLE, **FIG,** AND **NUT** STUFFING **MUFFINS**

Celebrate harvest time by combining crunchy red and green apples, nuts, and dried figs in this one-of-a-kind stuffing muffin.

1. Preheat the oven to 350°F. Liberally grease 12 muffin cups to the rims and set aside.

2. Combine the stuffing mix, apples, figs, walnuts or almonds, raisins (if desired), orange zest, and cinnamon in a large bowl. Stir in the apple juice and vegetable oil.

3. Spoon the batter into the muffin cups, dividing it evenly among the cups. Bake uncovered for 20 minutes or until golden brown.

4. Allow the muffins to rest in the cups for 5 minutes. Then run a knife around the rims to loosen the muffins, unmold, and serve.

YIELD: **12** SERVINGS

3 cups cornbread stuffing mix

2 apples (one red and one green), shredded with skin on

I cup chopped dried figs

$2/3$ cup chopped walnuts or almonds

2 tablespoons dark raisins, optional

Zest of I orange, minced

$1/4$ teaspoon ground cinnamon

I cup apple juice

$1/4$ cup vegetable oil

BACONANDAPRICOT
STUFFINGMUFFINS

*These muffins marry the smoky flavor of crisp bacon
with the tart chewiness of dried apricots. Delicious!*

YIELD: 12 SERVINGS

6 cups cornbread
stuffing mix

1 ½ cups chopped
dried apricots

½ cup crumbled crisp bacon
(about 8 ounces uncooked)

3 whole eggs, well beaten

1 ½ cups chicken broth

½ cup melted butter
or margarine

6 dried apricots, halved,
for garnish

1. Preheat the oven to 350°F. Liberally grease 12 muffin cups to the rims and set aside.

2. Combine the stuffing mix, apricots, and bacon in a large bowl. Stir in the eggs, chicken broth, and butter or margarine.

3. Spoon the batter into the muffin cups, dividing it evenly among the cups, and top each with a dried apricot half. Bake uncovered for 30 to 35 minutes, or until firm, covering the muffins with aluminum foil if the apricot garnish begins browning too quickly.

4. Allow the muffins to rest in the cups for 5 minutes. Then run a knife around the rims to loosen the muffins, unmold, and serve.

BROWN**RICE**AND**CASHEW** **STUFFING**MUFFINS

Brown rice is a perfect complement to cornbread stuffing,
while cashews add flavor and a delightful crunch.

YIELD: 12 SERVINGS

6 cups cornbread
stuffing mix

I cup cooked brown rice

I cup melted butter
or margarine

I cup cashew pieces

$\frac{1}{2}$ cup diced celery

2 teaspoons chopped
green onion

I $\frac{1}{4}$ cups water or broth

12 whole cashews
for garnish

1. Preheat the oven to 350°F. Liberally grease 12 muffin cups to the rims and set aside.

2. Combine the stuffing mix, rice, and butter or margarine in a large bowl. Stir in the cashew pieces, celery, and green onion. Then gradually stir in the water or broth, adding more if necessary to make the mixture hold together, but not so much that the mixture becomes soggy.

3. Spoon the batter into the muffin cups, dividing it evenly among the cups, and top each with a whole cashew. Bake uncovered for 20 to 25 minutes, or until lightly browned.

4. Allow the muffins to rest in the cups for 5 minutes. Then run a knife around the rims to loosen the muffins, unmold, and serve.

PUMPKINSTUFFING**BALLS**

The perfect addition to a Thanksgiving table,
these delicious treats are topped with crunchy walnuts.

3 cups seasoned
stuffing mix

$1/2$ cup melted butter
or margarine

I cup canned pumpkin

I teaspoon ground allspice

$3/4$ cup water

6 to 8 walnut halves

1. Preheat the oven to 325°F. Grease a casserole dish and set aside.

2. Combine the stuffing mix with the melted butter or margarine in a large bowl, and set aside.

3. Combine the pumpkin with the allspice in a small bowl. Stir the pumpkin mixture into the stuffing mixture. Then blend in the water, mixing well but lightly.

4. Shape the stuffing mixture into 6 to 8 balls. Press a walnut half on top of each ball so that the nut is half covered by the stuffing.

5. Arrange the stuffing balls in the prepared dish, cover tightly with aluminum foil, and bake for 35 to 45 minutes, or until firm to the touch.

PINEAPPLESTUFFINGBALLS

Featuring both chopped pineapple and pineapple juice, these stuffing balls are a wonderful complement to ham or pork chops.

YIELD: 6 TO 8 SERVINGS

3 cups cornbread stuffing mix

$^1/_2$ cup melted butter or margarine

I cup fresh or canned pineapple chopped into bite-size pieces, juice reserved

$^1/_2$ teaspoon ground cinnamon

$^1/_2$ cup pineapple juice

$^1/_4$ cup water

6 to 8 macadamia nuts, optional

1. Preheat the oven to 325°F. Grease a casserole dish and set aside.

2. Combine the stuffing mix with the melted butter or margarine in a large bowl, and set aside.

3. Combine the pineapple with the cinnamon in a small bowl. Blend the pineapple mixture with the stuffing. Then blend in the pineapple juice—including the juice that was drained from the pineapple pieces—and the water, mixing well but lightly.

4. Shape the stuffing mixture into 6 to 8 balls. If desired, press a macadamia nut on top of each ball so that the nut is half covered by the stuffing.

5. Arrange the stuffing balls in the prepared dish, cover tightly with aluminum foil, and bake for 35 to 45 minutes, or until firm to the touch.

GRAPEFRUITANDWALNUT STUFFINGBALLSWITH CITRUS-MINTSAUCE

YIELD: 6 TO 8 SERVINGS

3 cups cornbread
stuffing mix

I cup grapefruit
segments

$\frac{1}{2}$ cup chopped walnuts

$\frac{1}{4}$ cup chopped fresh mint

$\frac{1}{4}$ cup brown sugar

$\frac{1}{2}$ cup melted butter
or margarine

$\frac{3}{4}$ cup grapefruit juice

SAUCE

2 grapefruits, sectioned
and chopped into bite-size
pieces, juice reserved

$\frac{1}{2}$ cup apple cider

I $\frac{1}{2}$ tablespoons honey

I tablespoon cornstarch

$\frac{1}{2}$ teaspoon crushed
dried mint

2 $\frac{1}{2}$ tablespoons chopped
fresh mint for garnish

2 $\frac{1}{2}$ tablespoons grapefruit
zest for garnish

*These unique stuffing balls include tangy grapefruit
and walnuts, and are topped with a warm citrus sauce.*

1. Preheat the oven to 325°F. Spray a baking sheet with non-stick cooking spray and set aside.

2. Combine the stuffing mix, grapefruit segments, walnuts, mint, and brown sugar in a large bowl. Stir in first the melted butter and then the grapefruit juice, tossing lightly but thoroughly after each addition.

3. Shape the stuffing mixture into 6 to 8 balls and arrange on the prepared baking sheet. Cover and bake for 35 minutes, or until firm to the touch.

4. To make the sauce, set the grapefruit sections aside, and combine the reserved grapefruit juice, cider, honey, and cornstarch in a small saucepan. Bring the mixture to a boil over medium heat and boil for 4 minutes, stirring constantly as the mixture thickens. Stir in the grapefruit sections and the mint.

5. Serve the sauce warm over the stuffing balls, garnishing with the chopped mint and grapefruit zest.

PARMESANANDSPINACH
STUFFINGBALLS

*Parmesan and spinach make the perfect dinner companions
when combined in these outstanding stuffing balls.*

YIELD: 4 SERVINGS

1. Preheat the oven to 350°F.

2. Cook the spinach according to package instructions. Drain
   well and allow to cool.

3. Combine the cooled spinach with all of the remaining ingredients in a large bowl, mixing well.

4. Roll the stuffing mixture into walnut-sized balls, and arrange
   on an ungreased baking sheet. Bake uncovered for 15 minutes, or until lightly browned.

10-ounce package frozen
chopped spinach

1 cup seasoned
stuffing mix

1 medium onion, chopped

3 eggs, beaten

$\frac{1}{3}$ cup grated Parmesan
cheese

$\frac{1}{4}$ cup melted butter
or margarine

BROCCOLIANDCHEDDAR STUFFINGCROQUETTES

These croquettes deliciously combine broccoli and Cheddar with sweet cornbread stuffing. The resulting side dish is a wonderful accompaniment to almost any entrée.

YIELD: 8 SERVINGS

1-pound package frozen broccoli

1 ½ cups cornbread stuffing mix

1 ½ cups shredded Cheddar cheese

4 eggs, slightly beaten

¼ teaspoon garlic powder

¼ cup melted butter or margarine

1. Preheat the oven to 400°F. Spray a baking sheet with non-stick cooking spray and set aside.

2. Cook the broccoli according to package directions. Drain well, allow to cool, and mince.

3. Combine the minced broccoli with all of the remaining ingredients except the butter or margarine. Then stir in the butter or margarine.

4. Using a tablespoon, shape the stuffing mixture into eight 1½-inch ovals or cylinders, and arrange on the prepared baking sheet. Bake uncovered for 10 to 15 minutes, or until lightly browned.

STUFFING**SOUFFLÉS**

*Sophie Cubbison may have started her career by cooking
down-home meals for ranch hands, but as time went on,
she added many sophisticated dishes to her repertoire.
Included among them were these individual puffs
flavored with Cheddar, chives, and bacon.*

YIELD: 6 SERVINGS

3 cups cornbread
stuffing mix

1 cup hot milk

3 eggs, well beaten

1 cup grated sharp
Cheddar cheese

6 slices bacon, cooked
crisp and crumbled

2 tablespoons minced
fresh parsley

1 tablespoon chopped
fresh chives

1. Preheat the oven to 350°F. Liberally grease six 4-ounce (½ cup) custard cups and set aside.

2. Combine the stuffing mix with the hot milk in a large bowl. Set aside to cool.

3. Mix the eggs, cheese, bacon, parsley, and chives into the cooled stuffing mix.

4. Spoon the stuffing mixture into the prepared custard cups, dividing it equally, and bake uncovered for 35 to 40 minutes, or until puffed and brown.

NEAPOLITANSTUFFING "SANDWICHES"

Talk about stuffing taking on an innovative shape! In this recipe, seasoned stuffing mix, porcini mushrooms, sun-dried tomatoes, almonds, red onions, and olives combine to create a fantastic Neapolitan-style open sandwich.

YIELD: 8 SERVINGS

1/4 cup dried porcini mushrooms

Water or white wine, heated

6 cups seasoned stuffing mix

1/2 cup chopped marinated sun-dried tomatoes, with oil reserved

I cup finely chopped red onion

I cup finely chopped celery

1/2 cup chopped almonds

1/2 cup coarsely chopped Kalamata olives

1/2 cup coarsely chopped green olives

1 1/4 cups chicken broth

6 tablespoons Dijon mustard

8 tomato slices

Sprigs of fresh thyme for garnish

1. Preheat the oven to 350° F. Line both a 9-x-5-x-3-inch loaf pan and a baking sheet with aluminum foil, grease well, and set aside.

2. Place the mushrooms in a small bowl, cover with the hot water or wine, and allow to soak for 30 minutes. Carefully drain the liquid from the mushrooms, leaving any grit in the bowl, and add the liquid to the chicken broth. Finely chop the mushrooms and set aside.

3. Place the stuffing mix in a large bowl and set aside.

4. Place the reserved sun-dried tomato oil in a medium-sized skillet over medium heat. Add the onion and celery and sauté for 5 minutes, or until the vegetables are tender.

5. Add the sautéed vegetables to the stuffing mix and toss lightly. Stir in sun-dried tomatoes, almonds, and olives. Then pour in the chicken broth and blend lightly.

6. Transfer the stuffing mixture to the prepared loaf pan, packing the mixture in firmly. Cover tightly with aluminum foil and bake for 30 minutes or until firm to the touch.

7. Preheat the broiler. While the broiler is heating up, transfer the loaf pan to a cooling rack. When cool, remove the loaf from the pan, carefully peeling off the foil. Then, with a sharp knife, cut the loaf into 8 equal slices.

8. Arrange the slices on the prepared baking sheet and broil for 2 to 3 minutes, or until the tops are crusty and golden. Watch carefully to avoid burning.

9. Spread each slice lightly with the Dijon mustard, top with a slice of tomato, and garnish with a sprig of thyme.

CREAMEDCORNFRITTERS

*These tempting little cakes are crunchy on the outside
with a moist creamed corn filling. Delicious!*

YIELD: 6 SERVINGS
(2 FRITTERS EACH)

2 eggs, beaten

16-ounce can cream-style
corn, or 2 cups fresh
corn kernels plus
1/4 cup heavy cream

1 1/2 cups cornbread
stuffing mix

1 1/2 tablespoons chopped
green onions

1/4 teaspoon salt

Dash cayenne pepper

1/4 cup butter or margarine

1. Place the eggs in a large bowl. Stir in the corn and, if needed, the cream. Then stir in the stuffing mix, green onions, salt, and cayenne pepper.

2. Place the butter or margarine on a large griddle or skillet, and melt over medium-high heat. When the fat begins to sizzle, drop the corn mixture by tablespoonfuls onto the pan and cook for 2 to 3 minutes, or until the bottom is golden brown. Turn the fritters over with tongs or a spatula, and continue to cook until the second side is golden brown. Be careful not to burn the fritters.

9. **Stuffing**in **Disguise**

Sophie Cubbison could think outside the box—outside the stuffing box, that is. She knew that stuffing mix could do much more than fill a golden holiday bird. And as she used her seasoned Melba-toasted bread crumbs to make delicious meatloaf, lasagna, quiches, and more, friends, family, and colleagues also learned the versatility of stuffing mix.

This chapter provides nearly two dozen dishes that feature stuffing "in disguise." In some dishes, it makes a luscious filling for succulent artichokes or other vegetables. In others, it makes a seasoned crust for oven-fried chicken. Our Mock Lasagna shows how stuffing mix can replace pasta—and add more flavor than pasta ever could. And our Easy Cornbread Stuffing Tamales demonstrate how it can be used in a corn dough filling. However, nowhere is the versatility of stuffing mix more obvious than in our desserts. In an enticing apple crisp and a delectable maple yam pie, stuffing mix proves to be a superior replacement for flour and other baking ingredients. Who knew that stuffing mix could be used in so many ways?

Whether you use stuffing mix to form a fast crust, to soak up a home-made sauce, or to whip up a sweet and crunchy topping, you'll find that it blends with almost any ingredient you have in your cupboard, elevating old dishes to new heights. Soon, you'll be amazing your family with the limitless ways to serve "stuffing in disguise."

PECANANDPIMIENTO
STUFFEDMUSHROOMS

Stuffed mushrooms are always a crowd pleaser. Our version—
which includes pecans, pimiento, and vegetables—
might just result in a standing ovation.

**YIELD: 20 STUFFED
MUSHROOMS**

½ cup melted butter

½ cup chopped onion

½ cup chopped celery

½ cup chopped pecans

¼ cup chopped pimiento

3 cups cornbread
stuffing mix

1 ¼ cups beef broth

2 eggs, well beaten

20 large mushrooms

1. Preheat the oven to 350°F. Lightly grease a large shallow baking pan and set aside.

2. Place the butter in a large skillet over medium heat. Add the onion and celery and sauté for about 5 minutes, or until the vegetables are soft.

3. Add the pecans and pimiento to the onion mixture, stirring to combine. Stir in the stuffing mix, broth, and eggs, and remove from the heat.

4. Wash the mushrooms, dry, and remove the stems. Fill the caps with the stuffing mixture, dividing it evenly among the mushrooms. Arrange the stuffed mushrooms in the prepared baking pan.

5. Pour ¼ cup water into the bottom of the pan and bake uncovered for 20 minutes, or until the tops are lightly browned.

CAPERAND**GARLIC** STUFFED**ARTICHOKES**

Stuffing mix makes a delectably light and crispy filling for succulent artichokes. The addition of capers and julienned salami creates an especially memorable treat.

1. Preheat the oven to 350°F.

2. Trim the stem ends of the artichokes so that the artichokes will sit flat, and strip off any small outer leaves. Place the artichokes on a cutting board and with a sharp knife, cut about ¾ inch off the top of each. Firmly press the cut portion against the cutting board to loosen the leaves, and spread the leaves apart so that they will hold the stuffing mixture.

3. Combine the stuffing mix, parsley, salami, garlic, water or wine, and capers in a large bowl.

4. Using a spoon, force some of the stuffing mixture down to the heart of each artichoke and between the leaves. Fit the artichokes snugly into a deep casserole dish. Drizzle some of the oil over each artichoke, and pour the remaining oil into the dish. Pour the water into the dish and cover tightly with aluminum foil.

5. Bake for 45 minutes to 1 hour, or until a fork easily pierces the artichoke bottoms or a leaf can be easily pulled from the artichoke. Serve hot or at room temperature.

YIELD: 6 SERVINGS

6 large artichokes

1 ½ cups seasoned stuffing mix

¼ cup chopped fresh parsley

4 slices Italian dry salami, cut into julienne strips

2 cloves garlic, finely minced

2 tablespoons water or dry white wine

1 tablespoon capers, well drained

½ cup olive oil

½ cup water

MUSHROOM**QUICHE**WITH **STUFFING**CRUST

Once Sophie found that cornbread stuffing mix made a wonderful pie crust, she began concocting a variety of delectable dishes, including this creamy mushroom and onion quiche.

Y**YIELD: 8 SERVINGS**

CRUST

3 cups cornbread stuffing mix

¾ cup hot water

3 tablespoons melted butter or margarine

FILLING

2 tablespoons butter or margarine

I bunch green onions, chopped coarsely

8 ounces fresh mushrooms, sliced

3 eggs, beaten

1 ½ cups cream or milk

I cup grated Swiss or Monterey Jack cheese

Salt to taste

Freshly ground black pepper to taste

Ground nutmeg to taste

1. Preheat the oven to 350°F. Very lightly spray a 9-inch quiche pan or deep-dish pie pan with nonstick cooking spray and set aside.

2. To prepare the crust, combine the stuffing mix, hot water, and butter or margarine in a medium-sized bowl. Press the mixture against the bottom and sides of the prepared pan and bake for 20 minutes, or until golden brown. Remove from the oven and allow to cool.

3. To prepare the filling, place the butter or margarine in a large skillet and melt over medium heat. Add the green onions and mushrooms and sauté for about 5 minutes, or until the vegetables are soft. Set aside.

4. Combine all of the remaining filling ingredients in a large bowl. Stir in the sautéed vegetables.

5. Spoon the filling mixture into the cooled crust, and place on a flat baking pan to catch any spills. Bake for 45 to 50 minutes, or until the quiche seems set when shaken and a knife inserted near the edge comes out clean. Slice into thin appetizer-size slices or into entrée-size wedges.

TOMATOESAUGRATIN

Why should only potatoes be served au gratin, with a crunchy topping of buttered bread crumbs? In this delicious variation, juicy tomatoes are layered with a mixture of butter, sautéed onions and garlic, and stuffing mix, and then baked to crisp perfection.

YIELD: **6** SERVINGS

3 cups seasoned
stuffing mix

¹/₂ cup butter or margarine

1 large onion,
finely chopped

1 garlic clove, chopped

6 large tomatoes,
thinly sliced

Salt to taste

1. Preheat the oven to 350°F. Lightly spray a 2¹/₂-quart casserole dish with nonstick cooking spray and set aside.

2. Place the stuffing mix in a medium-sized bowl and set aside.

3. Place the butter or margarine in a small skillet, and melt over medium heat. Add the onion and garlic and sauté for about 5 minutes, or until golden.

4. Pour the contents of the skillet, including the butter or margarine, over the stuffing mix. Stir until blended.

5. Layer the tomatoes and the stuffing mixture in the prepared casserole dish, beginning and ending with a layer of the stuffing mixture. Sprinkle each layer of tomatoes lightly with salt as you go. Bake uncovered for 35 to 40 minutes, or until brown and crusty on top.

BREADEDCORN**SOUFFLÉ**

*Cornbread stuffing mix is the perfect foundation
for this hearty soufflé, which features
creamed corn and fresh onion and parsley.*

YIELD: 6 TO 8 SERVINGS

4 eggs, separated

3 cups cornbread
stuffing mix

14.75-ounce can
creamed corn

3 cups milk

$1/4$ cup finely chopped
onion

$1/4$ cup finely chopped
fresh parsley

$1/4$ cup melted butter
or margarine

1. Preheat the oven to 350°F. Liberally grease a 2$1/2$-quart casserole dish and set aside.

2. Set the egg yolks aside. Beat the whites until stiff, and set aside.

3. Combine the stuffing mix, creamed corn, milk, egg yolks, onion, parsley, and butter or margarine in a large bowl, mixing well with a fork. Fold in the egg whites.

4. Pour the corn mixture into the prepared dish and bake uncovered for 1 hour, or until puffed and brown.

CRUSTY**CABBAGE**WEDGES

*If you've never cared for cabbage, this dish will change
your mind forever. Sophie served up this nutritious
vegetable delectably flavored with a crisp topping of bacon,
Parmesan cheese, and seasoned stuffing mix.*

YIELD: 8 SERVINGS

1 teaspoon salt

1 large head cabbage

8 slices bacon, diced

3 cups cornbread
stuffing mix

$1/4$ cup grated
Parmesan cheese

1. Place 8 cups of water and the salt in a large saucepan, and bring to a boil.

2. While the water is coming to a boil, remove the tough outer leaves from the cabbage. Cut the cabbage into 8 wedges, but do not remove the core. Set aside.

3. Place the bacon in a large skillet, and cook over medium heat until crisp. Add the stuffing mix and cheese and continue cooking and stirring for about 3 minutes, or until the stuffing is brown and crisp. Keep warm.

4. Place the cabbage wedges in the boiling water and cook for about 5 minutes, or until tender.

5. Drain the cabbage and arrange the wedges on a platter. Top with the hot stuffing mixture.

SCANDINAVIAN-STYLE STUFFED**ZUCCHINI**

*During her travels around the world, Sophie enjoyed
a Scandinavian-style stuffed zucchini, which
she then recreated using stuffing mix.*

YIELD: 6 SERVINGS

3 large zucchini

¼ cup butter or margarine

1 small onion, chopped

3 cups cornbread
stuffing mix

2 hard boiled eggs,
chopped

½ cup tomato juice

¼ cup chopped
fresh parsley

6 strips bacon, cooked
but not crisp

1. Preheat the oven to 350°F.

2. Cut each zucchini in half lengthwise. Using a sharp knife or teaspoon, scoop out the center of each half, leaving a shell about ½-inch thick. Set aside the shells. Chop the removed zucchini and set aside.

3. Place the butter or margarine in a medium-sized skillet, and melt over medium heat. Add the chopped zucchini and onion and sauté for 5 minutes, or until the vegetables are soft.

4. Combine the stuffing mix and sautéed vegetables in a large bowl. Add the eggs, tomato juice, and parsley, and blend lightly. Stuff the reserved zucchini shells with the stuffing mixture, dividing the mixture evenly among the shells.

5. Place ½ inch of water in a shallow baking pan, and arrange the stuffed zucchini in the pan. Garnish each zucchini with a piece of bacon and bake uncovered for 35 to 40 minutes, or until the zucchini are easily pierced with a fork.

ZESTYBAKEDORANGES

*Stuffed oranges? Unusual, yes, but once you sample
these sweet and savory gems, you'll wonder why
oranges aren't always served this way!*

1. Preheat the oven to 350°F.

2. Cut the top off 6 of the oranges, reserving the tops. Cut a very thin slice off the bottom of each orange so it sits upright. With a knife and spoon, scoop out the pulp of the 6 oranges, chop the pulp, and place it in a large bowl. Set the orange shells aside.

3. Remove and chop the zest from the remaining orange, and place it in the bowl with the orange pulp. Discard the rest of the orange or keep for other uses.

4. Add the stuffing mix, onion, parsley, orange juice, and oil to the chopped orange, and mix with a spoon, adding more juice if necessary to achieve the desired moistness. Stuff the oranges with the mixture, top with the reserved orange tops, and wrap each individually in aluminum foil.

5. Arrange the wrapped oranges in a shallow baking dish and bake for 15 to 20 minutes or until thoroughly heated.

YIELD: 6 SERVINGS

7 oranges

3 cups seasoned or cornbread stuffing mix

$1/2$ red onion, finely chopped

$1/4$ cup finely chopped fresh parsley

1 cup orange juice

$1/4$ cup vegetable oil

OVEN-FRIEDCHICKEN

When Sophie was a teen cooking for ranch hands,
she made a mean fried chicken. Years later she improved her
recipe further by using crushed stuffing mix to coat the chicken.

YIELD: 4 SERVINGS

2 cups seasoned
stuffing mix

3-pound fryer, cut up

10.75-ounce can
condensed cream of
celery soup, divided

3/4 cup milk, divided

1 1/2 tablespoons chopped
fresh chives, divided

1 tablespoon chopped
fresh parsley

1/4 cup melted butter
or margarine

1. Preheat the oven to 400°F. Spray a shallow baking pan with nonstick cooking spray and set aside.

2. Place the stuffing mix in a plastic bag, seal, and use a rolling pin to crush the mix into fine crumbs. Transfer the crumbs to a shallow bowl and set aside.

3. Rinse the chicken pieces and pat dry. Set aside.

4. In a pie pan, mix together 1/3 cup of the soup, 1/4 cup of the milk, 1 tablespoon of the chives, and all of the parsley. Dip each chicken piece in the soup mixture. Then roll the piece in the crushed stuffing, pressing to coat.

5. Arrange the coated chicken pieces in the prepared baking pan, and drizzle with the melted butter or margarine. Bake uncovered for 45 minutes, or until a thermometer inserted in the chicken reads 170°F.

6. When the chicken is almost done, combine the remaining soup, milk, and chives in a small saucepan, and simmer over medium-low heat until piping hot. Serve drizzled over the chicken.

SPANISH**MEATLOAF**

*This easy-to-make meatloaf may be the best
you ever tasted. Green chile salsa gives it a kick,
and Monterey Jack cheese adds further flavor.*

1. Preheat the oven to 350°F. Lightly spray a 9-x-5-inch loaf pan with nonstick cooking spray and set aside.

2. Place the stuffing mix, salsa, eggs, and oregano in a large bowl, and stir to mix. Add the ground beef and blend thoroughly.

3. Transfer the beef mixture to the prepared loaf pan, smoothing the top, and bake uncovered for 1 to 1¼ hours, or until a meat thermometer inserted in the loaf reaches at least 160°F.

4. During the last few minutes of baking, cut each cheese slice diagonally to form 2 triangles and carefully arrange overlapping slices of cheese on top of the loaf. Continue baking just until the cheese begins to melt.

5. Remove the loaf from the oven and allow to sit for 5 minutes so that the juices are reabsorbed into the meat. If desired, garnish the top of the meatloaf with stuffed olives before serving.

YIELD: 8 TO 10 SERVINGS

3 cups cornbread stuffing mix

¾ cup green chile salsa

2 eggs

½ teaspoon dried oregano, crushed

2 pounds ground round or chuck

3 slices Monterey Jack cheese

Stuffed green olives for garnish (optional)

MOCK**LASAGNA**

YIELD: **6** SERVINGS

¾ cup butter or margarine, divided

2 large onions, chopped

2 cloves garlic, minced

I pound ground round or sirloin

14.5-ounce can diced tomatoes

2 tablespoons chopped fresh chives

Salt to taste

Freshly ground black pepper to taste

Crushed dried oregano to taste

6 cups seasoned stuffing mix

I cup water

2 eggs, well beaten

I pound mozzarella cheese, sliced

½ cup grated Parmesan cheese

I pound ricotta cheese

In this tasty take on lasagna, stuffing mix brilliantly replaces pasta and soaks up a delightful homemade tomato-meat sauce. Three cheeses add flavor and creaminess to the dish.

1. Preheat the oven to 350°F. Liberally grease a 9-x-13-x-2-inch baking dish and set aside.

2. Place ¼ cup of the butter or margarine in a large skillet, and melt over medium heat. Add the onions and garlic and sauté for 5 minutes, or until the vegetables are golden.

3. Add the ground beef to the skillet and cook, stirring to break the meat up, for about 5 minutes, or until the meat is browned and no pink remains. Stir in the tomatoes and chives, remove from the heat, and season to taste with salt, pepper, and oregano. Set aside.

4. Place the remaining ½ cup of butter in a small saucepan and melt over low heat. Combine the stuffing mix, butter, water, and eggs in a large bowl.

5. Spread a third of the stuffing mixture over the bottom of the prepared baking dish. Top with half of the meat mixture, a third of the mozzarella cheese, a third of the Parmesan cheese, and half of the ricotta cheese. Top with half of the remaining stuffing mixture, the remainder of the meat mixture, half of the remaining mozzarella cheese, half of the remaining Parmesan cheese, and the remainder of the ricotta cheese. Top with the remainder of the stuffing mixture, the mozzarella cheese, and the Parmesan cheese.

6. Cover the dish and bake for 15 minutes. Remove the cover and bake for 45 additional minutes, or until the top is light brown and melted. Allow to sit for 10 minutes before cutting into squares and serving.

TURKEY-STUFFED**EGGPLANT**

Eggplant has the ability to soak up all of the wonderful flavors around it. In this dish, it is sautéed with garlic and onion and lovingly mixed with other luscious ingredients before being baked. Delicious!

YIELD: **6** SERVINGS

3 eggplants, each about 12 ounces

2 tablespoons vegetable oil

¼ cup butter or margarine

1 medium onion, chopped

1 green bell pepper, chopped

1 stalk celery, chopped

1 clove garlic, minced

1 ½ teaspoons dried basil, crushed

1 ½ teaspoons dried oregano, crushed

1 ¼ teaspoons salt

½ teaspoon freshly ground black pepper

2 cups cubed cooked turkey

2 tablespoons chopped fresh parsley

½ cup poultry gravy

3 tablespoons grated Parmesan cheese

½ cup chicken broth

1. Preheat the oven to 350°F.

2. To prepare the stuffing mixture, place the butter or margarine in a large saucepan, and melt over medium heat. Add the celery and onion and sauté for 5 minutes, or until the vegetables are soft.

3. Add the broth, fruit juice, or water to the pan, and bring to a boil over high heat. Cover the saucepan, reduce the heat, and simmer for 3 minutes.

4. Set aside 2 tablespoons of the stuffing mix. Remove the saucepan from the heat and stir in the remaining mix. Cover and let stand for 3 to 5 minutes, or until the liquid has been absorbed. Set aside.

5. Cut each eggplant in half lengthwise and scoop out the flesh, leaving a shell ½- to ¾-inch thick, and reserving the eggplant that has been scooped out. Coarsely chop the flesh and set aside. Cut a thin slice from the bottom of each eggplant half so that it stands upright. Arrange the shells in a baking dish, brush with the oil, and bake for 20 minutes.

6. While the shells are baking, place the butter or margarine in a large skillet and melt over low-medium heat. Add the reserved chopped eggplant, onion, green pepper, celery, and garlic, and sauté for about 5 minutes, or just until tender, stirring often. Stir in the basil, oregano, salt, and pepper.

7. Remove the skillet from the heat and stir in the prepared stuffing mixture, turkey, and parsley. Moisten lightly with the gravy. Then divide the mixture among the 6 eggplant shells, piling the mixture into each shell.

8. Combine the Parmesan with the reserved dry stuffing mix in a small bowl. Sprinkle the mixture evenly over the stuffed eggplants, and arrange in the baking dish.

9. Pour the chicken broth into the bottom of the dish, cover, and bake for 15 minutes. Uncover the dish and bake for 15 additional minutes, or until the shells are tender. Serve with additional Parmesan cheese for sprinkling.

STUFFING MIXTURE

$\frac{1}{2}$ cup butter or margarine

$\frac{1}{2}$ cup finely chopped celery

$\frac{1}{2}$ cup finely chopped onion

$\frac{1}{2}$ cup chicken broth, fruit juice, or water

3 cups seasoned or cornbread stuffing mix

STUFFIN'-**STUFFED CABBAGE**ROLLS

This twist on classic stuffed cabbage saves time by blending savory cornbread stuffing mix with flavorful diced ham, rather than the usual ground meat.

**YIELD: 4 SERVINGS
(2 ROLLS EACH)**

1/4 cup butter or margarine

1/4 cup chopped onion

1/4 cup chopped celery

1 cup diced ham

3/4 cup chicken broth

3 cups cornbread stuffing mix

8 large cabbage leaves

1 cup tomato sauce

1/2 teaspoon dried basil, crushed

1. Preheat the oven to 350°F. Lightly spray a shallow baking pan with nonstick cooking spray and set aside.

2. Place the butter or margarine in a large skillet, and melt over medium heat. Add the onion and celery and sauté for 5 minutes, or until the vegetables are soft but not browned. Add the ham and cook for 3 additional minutes, or until the ham is lightly browned. Stir in the chicken broth.

3. Place the stuffing mix in a large bowl. Add the ham mixture and toss well to combine. Set aside.

4. Place 3 quarts of water and 1 tablespoon of salt in a large pot, and bring to a boil. Add the cabbage leaves, lower the heat, and simmer for 5 minutes, or until the leaves have softened. Carefully remove the leaves and drain well.

5. To make the rolls, place a cabbage leaf on a flat surface. Divide the stuffing mixture into 8 portions and place a portion in the center of each leaf. Fold the left and right sides over the filling, and then roll up the leaf. Repeat with the remaining leaves.

6. Arrange the stuffed cabbage leaves seam sides down and close together in the prepared baking pan. Cover and bake for 20 minutes.

7. While the cabbage is baking, combine the tomato sauce and basil in a small bowl. Spoon the sauce over the cabbage rolls and cook uncovered for 10 to 15 additional minutes, or until the cabbage is tender.

TURKEYAND CORNBREAD**SALAD**

In this salad, some of the stuffing mix is allowed to deliciously soak up the dressing, while the rest provides a crunchy topping.

1. Combine ¾ cup of the stuffing mix and all of the remaining ingredients in a large bowl, tossing to mix well. Cover and refrigerate for 4 hours or overnight.

2. Before serving, top the salad with the remaining ¼ cup of stuffing mix.

YIELD: 4 SERVINGS

1 cup cornbread stuffing mix, divided

2 cups cooked turkey, cut into ½-inch cubes

½ cup canned whole kernel corn, drained

¼ cup finely chopped green bell pepper

¼ cup finely chopped onion

¼ cup chopped pimiento

½ cup bottled or homemade ranch or blue cheese salad dressing

SHRIMP-**STUFFED** **BELL**PEPPERS

These bell pepper boats—stuffed with shrimp, chicken, cheese,
and seasoned stuffing mix—make a satisfying lunch
or a wonderfully light dinner entrée.

YIELD: 8 SERVINGS

8 equal-sized bell peppers,
any color

$1/_2$ cup butter or margarine

I pound skinless, boneless
chicken breast, cubed

I pound uncooked shrimp,
peeled, deveined,
and diced

Salt to taste

Freshly ground black pepper
to taste

3 cups seasoned
stuffing mix

I $1/_2$ cups hot chicken broth

I tablespoon paprika

$3/_4$ cup grated Cheddar
cheese

$3/_4$ cup grated Monterey
Jack cheese

1. Preheat the oven to 350°F. Spray a shallow baking dish with nonstick cooking spray and set aside.

2. Cut off and discard the top of each pepper to create a deep bowl, and remove the seeds and membranes. Wash well and set aside to dry.

3. Place the butter or margarine in a large skillet, and melt over low heat. Add the chicken and cook, stirring constantly, until the chicken is white. Add the shrimp, salt, and pepper, and cook until the shrimp turns pink. Remove from the heat and set aside.

4. Combine the stuffing mix and broth in a large bowl. Add the chicken mixture and the paprika, and mix well. If the mixture is not moist, add a little additional chicken broth or water. Taste and correct the seasoning if necessary.

5. Fill each pepper ¾ full with the stuffing mixture, and arrange the peppers in the prepared baking dish. Cover and bake for 30 minutes, or until the peppers are tender when pierced with the tip of a knife.

6. While the peppers are cooking, combine the cheeses in a small bowl. A few minutes before the peppers are done, remove them from the oven and top each with a couple of tablespoons of cheese. Return the peppers to the oven and heat for 5 additional minutes, or until the cheese is melted.

SOPHIE'SEASY**APPLE**CRISP

*This apple crisp is so easy to prepare and so delicious
that it is sure to become a family favorite.*

YIELD: 8 SERVINGS

6 cups seasoned
stuffing mix

1 cup melted butter

1 cup firmly packed
brown sugar

1 $\frac{1}{2}$ teaspoons ground
cinnamon

$\frac{1}{2}$ teaspoon ground nutmeg

6 tart apples, peeled, cored,
and thinly sliced

$\frac{1}{2}$ cup sugar

Heavy cream, whipped cream,
or vanilla ice cream

1. Preheat the oven to 350°F. Liberally grease a 9- or 10-inch-square baking pan with butter and set aside.

2. Combine the stuffing mix, butter, brown sugar, and spices in a large bowl. Arrange half of the mixture evenly over the bottom of the prepared baking pan. Top with all of the apple slices, sprinkle with the sugar, and cover with the remaining stuffing mixture.

3. Cover and bake for 15 minutes. Uncover the dish and bake for 20 additional minutes, or until the apples are easily pierced with a fork. Serve warm with heavy cream, whipped cream, or vanilla ice cream.

EASY**CORNBREAD** **STUFFING**TAMALES

Sophie was proud of her mother's Mexican heritage, and always enjoyed Mexican cooking. It was therefore fitting that she would use her cornbread stuffing mix to deliciously replace the corn dough usually used in the preparation of tamales.

YIELD: **6 SERVINGS** **(2 TAMALES EACH)**

6 cups cornbread stuffing mix

I cup chopped black olives

I cup whole kernel corn

I cup olive oil

I cup spicy tomato juice

$1/2$ cup green chile salsa

$1/4$ cup canned chopped jalapeño peppers

$1/4$ cup grated Pecorino Romano or Monterey Jack cheese

2 cups diced cooked turkey (optional)

12 dried corn husks, soaked in warm water for I hour

1. Place all of the ingredients except for the corn husks in a large bowl, and stir to mix well. Divide the mixture into 12 equal portions.

2. To make the tamales, remove a corn husk from the water and pat it dry. Lay the husk on a flat surface and place one portion of the filling in the center, forming it into a rectangular pillow on the husk. Bring the two long sides of the corn husk over the filling and overlap them a bit. Then fold the two remaining ends over the top of the husk. Repeat with the remaining husks.

3. Place the tamales folded sides down in a steamer basket, and place the basket over boiling water. Cover the pot and steam for 30 minutes, adding more water to the steamer as necessary to keep it from boiling out.

MAPLE YAM PIE

Pumpkin pie may become yesterday's news after you
sample this to-die-for maple yam confection!

YIELD: **8** SERVINGS

CRUST

3 cups cornbread stuffing mix

½ cup melted butter

½ cup apple juice

FILLING

29-ounce can yams, drained and cut into small pieces

½ cup butter, softened

2 eggs

¾ cup light brown sugar

½ cup maple syrup

½ cup heavy cream

2 tablespoons white wine

1 tablespoon lemon juice

1 tablespoon vanilla extract

½ teaspoon ground nutmeg

1 teaspoon ground cinnamon

½ teaspoon salt

1. Preheat the oven to 350°F. Lightly grease a 9-inch pie pan and set aside.

2. To prepare the crust, combine the stuffing mix, melted butter, and apple juice in a medium-sized bowl. Press the stuffing mixture evenly against the bottom and sides of the pie pan and bake for 15 minutes, or until lightly browned. Remove the crust from the oven and allow to cool.

3. To prepare the filling, place the yams in a large bowl, and whip with an electric mixer until smooth. Whip in the butter, eggs, brown sugar, maple syrup, cream, white wine, lemon juice, vanilla extract, nutmeg, cinnamon, and salt.

4. Pour the yam mixture into the pie shell and bake uncovered for 30 minutes, or until the filling is set and just barely crisp on top. Serve warm or at room temperature.

METRIC CONVERSION TABLES

COMMON LIQUID CONVERSIONS

Measurement	=	Milliliters
1/4 teaspoon	=	1.25 milliliters
1/2 teaspoon	=	2.50 milliliters
3/4 teaspoon	=	3.75 milliliters
1 teaspoon	=	5.00 milliliters
1 1/4 teaspoons	=	6.25 milliliters
1 1/2 teaspoons	=	7.50 milliliters
1 3/4 teaspoons	=	8.75 milliliters
2 teaspoons	=	10.0 milliliters
1 tablespoon	=	15.0 milliliters
2 tablespoons	=	30.0 milliliters

Measurement	=	Liters
1/4 cup	=	0.06 liters
1/2 cup	=	0.12 liters
3/4 cup	=	0.18 liters
1 cup	=	0.24 liters
1 1/4 cups	=	0.30 liters
1 1/2 cups	=	0.36 liters
2 cups	=	0.48 liters
2 1/2 cups	=	0.60 liters
3 cups	=	0.72 liters
3 1/2 cups	=	0.84 liters
4 cups	=	0.96 liters
4 1/2 cups	=	1.08 liters
5 cups	=	1.20 liters
5 1/2 cups	=	1.32 liters

CONVERTING FAHRENHEIT TO CELSIUS

Fahrenheit	=	Celsius
200–205	=	95
220–225	=	105
245–250	=	120
275	=	135
300–305	=	150
325–330	=	165
345–350	=	175
370–375	=	190
400–405	=	205
425–430	=	220
445–450	=	230
470–475	=	245
500	=	260

CONVERSION FORMULAS

LIQUID		
When You Know	Multiply By	To Determine
teaspoons	5.0	milliliters
tablespoons	15.0	milliliters
fluid ounces	30.0	milliliters
cups	0.24	liters
pints	0.47	liters
quarts	0.95	liters

WEIGHT		
When You Know	Multiply By	To Determine
ounces	28.0	grams
pounds	0.45	kilograms

Index

KITCHEN QUICKIES
Great, Satisfying Meals in Minutes
Marie Caratozzolo and Joanne Abrams

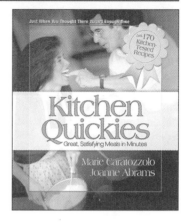

Ever feel that there aren't enough hours in the day to enjoy life's pleasures? Whether you're dealing with problems on the job, chasing after kids on the home front, or simply running from errand to errand, the evening probably finds you longing for a great meal, but without the time to prepare one.

Kitchen Quickies offers a solution. Virtually all of its over 170 kitchen-tested recipes—yes, really kitchen tested—call for a maximum of only five main ingredients other than kitchen staples, and each dish takes just minutes to prepare! Imagine being able to whip up dishes like Southwestern Tortilla Pizzas, Super Salmon Burgers, and Tuscan-Style Fusilli—in no time flat! As a bonus, these delicious dishes are actually good for you—low in fat and high in nutrients!

So the next time you think that there's simply no time to cook a great meal, pick up *Kitchen Quickies.* Who knows? You may even have time for a few "quickies" of your own.

$14.95 US / $22.50 CAN • 240 pages • 7.5 x 9-inch quality paperback • Full-color photos • Cooking • ISBN 0-7570-0085-1

THE SOURDOUGH BREAD BOWL COOKBOOK
For Parties, Holiday Celebrations, Family Gatherings, and Everyday Meals
John Vrattos and Lisa Messinger

For decades, tens of thousands of visitors to San Francisco's famed Fisherman's Wharf have enjoyed the sublime taste of crusty sourdough bread bowls filled with piping hot chowder. As the popularity of this culinary treat grew, so did the many creative uses of Sourdough Bread Bowls—from party centerpieces filled with luscious dips to edible settings for salads, entrées, and more. To answer the question, "How do I get started?" gourmet chef John Vrattos and best-selling food writer Lisa Messinger have created a cookbook that provides all the answers.

John and Lisa first guide the reader through the process of carving out a bread bowl that is beautiful and functional. From there, John and Lisa offer dozens and dozens of sumptuous kitchen-tested recipes, ranging from well-loved traditional dishes such as San Francisco's famed Clam Chowder to the innovative Warm Baja Shrimp Taco Dip. Throughout the book, you'll also find outstanding recipes specially developed by chefs at top American restaurants.

Whether you're hosting a Superbowl party, having the family over for dinner, or simply cooking up an intimate supper for two, make your event a little more special with *The Sourdough Bread Bowl Cookbook.*

$14.95 US / $22.50 CAN • 144 Pages • 7.5 x 7.5-inch quality paperback • Cooking / Bread Bowls • ISBN 0-7570-0149-1

THE MASON JAR COOKIE COOKBOOK
How to Create Mason Jar Cookie Mixes
Lonnette Parks

Nothing gladdens the heart like the tantalizing aroma of cookies baking in the oven. But for so many people, a busy lifestyle has made it impossible to find the time to bake at home—until now. Lonnette Parks, cookie baker extraordinaire, has not only developed fifty kitchen-tested recipes for delicious cookies, but has found a way for you to give the gift of home baking to everyone on your gift list.

For each mouth-watering cookie, the author provides the full recipe so that you can bake a variety of delights at home. In addition, she presents complete instructions for beautifully arranging the nonperishable ingredients in a Mason jar so that you can give the jar to a friend. By adding just a few common ingredients, your friend can then prepare fabulous home-baked cookies in a matter of minutes. Recipes include Best Ever Chocolate Chip Cookies, Blondies, and much, much more.

Whether you want to bake scrumptious cookies in your own kitchen or you'd like to give distinctive Mason jar cookie mixes to cookie-loving friends and family, *The Mason Jar Cookie Cookbook* is the perfect book.

$12.95 US / $21.00 CAN • 144 pages • 7.5 x 7.5-inch quality paperback • 2-Color • Cooking/Baking/Cookies • ISBN 0-7570-0046-0

THE MASON JAR SOUP-TO-NUTS COOKBOOK
How to Create Mason Jar Recipe Mixes
Lonnette Parks

In this follow-up to her best-selling book, *The Mason Jar Cookie Cookbook,* author and cook Lonnette Parks presents recipes for over fifty delicious soups, muffins, breads, cakes, pancakes, beverages, and more. And, just as in her previous book, the author tells you how to give the gift of home cooking to friends and family.

For each Mason jar creation, the author provides the full recipe so that you can cook and bake a variety of delights at home. In addition, she includes complete instructions for beautifully arranging the nonperishable ingredients in a Mason jar so that you can give the jar to a friend. Recipes include Golden Corn Bread, Double Chocolate Biscotti, Ginger Muffins, Apple Cinnamon Pancakes, Barley Rice Soup, Viennese Coffee, and much, much more.

$12.95 US / $21.00 CAN • 144 pages • 7.5 x 7.5-inch quality paperback • 2-Color • Cooking/ Crafts • ISBN 0-7570-0129-7

For more information about our books, visit our website at
www.squareonepublishers.com

FOR A COPY OF OUR CATALOG, CALL TOLL FREE: 877-900-BOOK, ext. 100